In the Know...
SAS®
Tips
& Techniques

From Around the Globe

Phil Mason

Ssas. | SAS Publishing

Table of Contents

Chapter 13 SCL 201

Chapter 14 FRAME Entries 225

Acknowledgments

I would like to acknowledge the assistance of various people in the production of this book. Mark Bodt actually contributed the full text of eight of the FRAME and SCL tips in this book. Other tips have emerged from discussion, either in person or over the Internet with other users.

I must especially thank the SAS-L Internet user group community on whom I tried many of my tips. Their comments and feedback have been very useful.

I would also like to thank:

- Michael H. Smith, who managed this publishing project, and Elizabeth Malcom, copyeditor (SAS Institute, USA)

- Mark Bodt who contributed some tips (Sunken Treasure Software Systems, New Zealand)

- Don Stanley who reviewed my draft and provided some useful information (Information Power, New Zealand)

- Glen Walker who answered lots of my FRAME and SCL questions (SAS Institute, USA)

- John Whittington who has provided some useful insights (Mediscience, England)

- My wife Esther who "beared with me" throughout the writing of this book.

Introduction

Welcome

Welcome to my first book and thanks for buying it. This book started out its life as a series of daily tips which I sent out to the Internet SAS user group, SAS-L. After sending out tips for about a year I had an idea for a daily calendar in which the SAS user could receive a new tip each day. This idea gradually evolved into a book which includes some tips already put out on SAS-L and many new tips.

How this book is organized

This book is arranged into chapters which contain collections of related tips. Each chapter also contains a reference to related documentation which you can refer to for further information.

The tips within each chapter are arranged in order from the most general to the most specific. Of course this is a very subjective decision and you may disagree with my ordering. My aim in ordering the tips this way is to make the most useful tips available to the reader first. Remember that if you are searching for a tip on a particular subject then look in the table of contents or the index, since this may take you right to the desired tip.

There is a common organization for each tip. Each tip contains the text of the tip and several other optional sections (such as, code examples, restrictions, and output) to help you to grasp the meaning quickly.

Sample Tip

How to determine which operating system you are using

 This allows a program to detect the operating system platform on which it is running and take appropriate action.

The automatic macro variable SYSSCP provides an abbreviation of the operating system on which SAS is running. However the new macro variable in SAS 6.11 called SYSSCPL returns the specific operating system.

This can be very useful when writing portable applications which take advantage of operating system specifics.

```
%put sysscp returns &sysscp ;
%put sysscpl returns &sysscpl ;
```

```
371   %put sysscp returns &sysscp ;
sysscp returns WIN
372   %put sysscpl returns &sysscpl ;
sysscpl returns WIN_95
```

 Since different values are returned on different platforms, you must handle potentially unknown values when using this macro variable--unless your code will only ever be used on certain platforms.

For more information

See *SAS Software: Changes and Enhancements, Release 6.11.*

Where to find more tips

Apart from tips and discussion that takes place on the SAS-L Internet user group, there are many other sources of good SAS tips. Many tips come right from the pages of SAS manuals. Apart from reading obscure parts of the basic manuals (*SAS Language: Reference, Version 6, First Edition, SAS Procedures Guide, Version 6, Third Edition*) a gold mine of tips can be found in SAS Technical Reports. I think that probably the best general technical report is P-222 which covers *Changes and Enhancements to Base SAS Software, Release 6.07* (345 pages). If you don't have it, I suggest you get it.

Another very useful book (devoted to SAS tips) is *SAS Programming Tips: A Guide to Efficient SAS Processing* (155 pages). Here is an extract from Page 132 of it...

Tips that are always useful

■ Read selection fields first

■ Write conditions in order of descending probability

■ Take advantage of output data sets

■ Sort data only when necessary

■ Sort as few observations and variables as possible

■ Examine raw data before reading them

■ Always specify SAS data set names

Note: the book contains full explanations and examples for these and MANY other tips.

If you have access to the Internet and have not subscribed to SAS-L then do so. This is an amazing resource for tips and technical advice from other SAS users around the world.

Chapter 1
A Collection of Useful Tips

How to fix unbalanced quotes

Sometimes when using lots of character strings and/or comments you may get your SAS code a little confused, ending up with messages like:

CHARACTER STRING WAS MORE THAN 200 CHARACTERS

This indicates that you may have unbalanced quotes. To close unbalanced quotes or comments, submit:

```
*'; *"; */;
```

This closes any unbalanced quotes or /* comments, and the statements are three harmless comments if no such unbalanced strings exist.

If things still don't work and if you are using macros, submit:

```
*); */; /*'*/ /*"*/; %mend;
```

This will close an unclosed macro argument list, close unbalanced quotes inside a macro (quotes and comments work differently inside macros), and terminate an unclosed macro definition.

If things still don't work, hit the ATTENTION/BREAK/INTERRUPT key. This key varies depending on your operating system and hardware being used. For instance, in Windows you can generally hold down the control key and then press the break key. Please refer to the documentation for your operating system.

If nothing happens, hit the RETURN or SUBMIT key. Do NOT hit the ATTENTION/BREAK/INTERRUPT key again, since that may kill the SAS session. You should get a message like this:

Press

Y to cancel submitted statements,
N to continue.

Carefully press Y and on some systems RETURN. This should return the tokenizer to a pristine state. If it doesn't, you have found a bug. Remember that the ultimate "fix" is to enter the ENDSAS or BYE command. This will close SAS so that you can restart it in a normal state.

Using a wildcard in variable lists

Using a wildcard in variable lists can save you a lot of typing and make your code much more generic (in some instances).

The colon can be used as a wildcard in variable lists. For example, ABC: means all variable names beginning with ABC.

```
data x(keep=a:) ;
   a1=1 ;
   a2=10 ;
   a3=100 ;
   b1=1000 ;
   b2=10000 ;
run;
```

```
The data set WORK.X has 1 observations and 3 variables.
The DATA statement used 0.01 CPU seconds and 1435K.
```

Notice that the three variables starting with the letter 'a' have been kept. We can also use 'a:' in procedures.

```
proc print ;
   var a:;
run ;
```

```
The PROCEDURE PRINT used 0.01 CPU seconds and 1489K.
```

The colon must be at the end of the name, not embedded—AB:C is invalid. Colons can be used in most places where other abbreviated variable lists, such as ABC1-ABC99, are allowed. It cannot be used in a SUM function in place of a list of variables.

Using wildcards to read external files

To read many identically laid-out and consecutively-named files (for example, Tab1.dat, tab2.dat, and so on) in a single DATA step in Release 6.08 and higher under Windows, Windows NT, VMS or OS/2 (not MVS or CMS), you can use the FILENAME statement with a wildcard (asterisk or question mark).

```
filename in 'c:\tab*.dat' ;

data report ;
   infile in ;
   input a b c ;
run ;
```

Commenting out code containing comments

Why?

Sometimes it is necessary to comment out an entire section of code, including DATA steps, procedures and other comments (of the /* */ kind). Traditional /* */ symbols will not work to comment out the code if there are other comments of that type in the code you want to comment out.

You can make a whole section of code into a macro, which will effectively comment it out. Be careful not to comment out code that contains a macro definition; otherwise, this technique may not work as expected, since the %MEND that you add may end the other macro. For example,

```
%macro junk ; * this statement used to comment out following
code ;

* do the next data step ;
data this ;    /* this is a nice dataset */
   set that ;
   x+1 ;          /* add 1 to x */

%mend ;   this statement used to comment out previous code ;
```

If you are using the macro statements to comment out a block of code, you can make the log more readable by using the NOSOURCE option to stop your commented out code from printing to the log.

```
options nosource;
%put **;
%put ** note: excluding some code. be back soon.;
%put **;
%macro junk ; * this statement used to comment out following
code ;
```

```
* do the next data step ;
data this ;    /* this is a nice dataset */
   set that ;
  x+1 ;                /* add 1 to x */

%mend ; this statement used to comment out previous code ;
options source;
```

Another possibility is to enforce the use of the "* ;" statement for all comments in open code. Then the "/* */" form can be reserved for commenting out large blocks of code. This technique requires that programmers observe this coding standard, since if they don't, you can get undesired results.

Sizing the screen space used by SAS applications

When using SAS interactively, it is usually desirable to maximize the space available to your application. This tip explains how to do so automatically.

The SAS Application Workspace (AWS) window can be sized and its menu bar turned off when you run an application in SAS (under Windows or OS/2). This is useful to ensure that maximum screen space is available for the application. Putting the following lines into your SAS configuration file (usually CONFIG.SAS) or on the SAS command line will accomplish this.

Part of CONFIG.SAS

```
* cause SAS to use 100% of the display area
* turn off the AWS menu bar.
Part of CONFIG.SAS
-awsdef 0 0 100 100
-noawsmenu
```

Data encryption for the beginner

The data stored in some SAS data sets is sensitive and needs protection. This tip provides sufficient protection for many security requirements.

If you don't yet have Release 6.11 of the SAS System, which has a built in data encryption feature, or if you are looking for further data encryption techniques, then this tip may be for you.

The BXOR function, added to base SAS in Release 6.07, presents budding encrypters with a basic tool for encrypting numbers. The function works by returning the result of a binary exclusive OR between the 2 arguments. The example below shows how a 'key' can be used to change 'original' numbers into 'coded' numbers. Then by doing a BXOR against those 'coded' numbers with the same key, the numbers are returned to the 'original' value.

This technique truncates values to the nearest 1 (see the value '34.4' in the example program below). If using decimal places (for example, money) then you should convert numbers to INTEGERS (for example, express the value in cents).

If you want to see what is going on a little better, you can use the following format to see where the bits are set in keys and data. This will enable you to easily check the function by hand.

Format	Description	Width Range	Default Width	Alignment
BINARYw.	converts numeric values to binary	1-64	8	left

```
data coded ;
  * set the value of the key ;
  retain key 1234567 ;
  format key original coded binary.;
  input original ;
  * encode the original value using the key ;
  coded=bxor(original,key);
  put key= original= coded= ;
  cards ;
1
1234567
999999
34.4
0
run ;
```

```
data decode ;
 * the value of the key must be the same,
   or else the number will not decode correctly ;
  retain key 1234567 ;
  set coded ;
 * decode the coded value using the key ;
  decoded=bxor(coded,key);
  put coded= decoded= ;
run ;
```

The following log shows the results of the first DATA step, which encodes the numbers.

```
KEY=1234567 ORIGINAL=1          CODED=1234566
KEY=1234567 ORIGINAL=1234567 CODED=0
KEY=1234567 ORIGINAL=999999   CODED=1938616
KEY=1234567 ORIGINAL=34.4      CODED=1234597
KEY=1234567 ORIGINAL=0          CODED=1234567
NOTE: The data set WORK.CODED has 5 observations and 3 vari-
ables.
NOTE: The DATA statement used 0.01 CPU seconds and 1451K.
```

The following log shows the results of the second DATA step, which decodes the numbers.

```
CODED=1234566 DECODED=1
CODED=0        DECODED=1234567
CODED=1938616 DECODED=999999
CODED=1234597 DECODED=34
CODED=1234567 DECODED=0
NOTE: The data set WORK.DECODE has 5 observations and 4 vari-
ables.
NOTE: The DATA statement used 0.01 CPU seconds and 1471K.
```

Capturing screens under Windows

There are many times when you might like to capture a screen image from SAS, such as when documenting SAS/AF applications.

Pressing ALT-PRTSCR under Windows 3.1 or Windows 95 captures the current screen and drops its graphic image into the clipboard, allowing pasting into applications such as Microsoft Word and Microsoft PowerPoint.

If there is a pop-up menu on the screen, then pressing ALT is considered to be a response to the pop-up menu, which means the pop-up menu disappears before the screen image is captured. However holding down PRTSCR and then pressing ALT will do a screen print with the pop-up menu intact.

Cautions in dealing with missing values

Here are several things to be aware of when dealing with missing values.

1. Most operators propagate missing values, but comparison operators treat them as negative infinity, so X<0 is true when X is missing.

2. Adding and/or subtracting several numbers using the plus (+) and minus (-) operators will return a missing value if any of the numbers are missing. To get around this, you should use the SUM function. The SUM function will only return a missing value if all of the values/variables being added are missing. If you always want a 0 returned, rather than a missing value, use SUM(0,var1,var2,...).

3. Many procedures (for example, SUMMARY, TABULATE, FREQ, CALENDAR, and so on) ignore missing values or at least treat them in a different way. Usually, missing values are ignored by default, and you should override the default if you want them included.

4. Some procedures have different statistics for missing and non-missing variables. For instance, PROC SUMMARY has N for the number of non-missing observations and NMISS for the number of observations with missing values. If you use PROC MEANS with a CLASS statement, you can get the NOBS statistic, which is the sum of missing and non-missing observations.

```
data _null_ ;
  * Initialise values ;
   a=. ;
   b=0 ;
   c=-7 ;
   d=99 ;
  * Try various forms of addition involving missing values ;
   add=a+b+c+d ;
   put 'Addition of missing & non-missing values :  ' add= ;
   sum=sum(a,b,c,d) ;
   put 'Sum of missing & non-missing values :  ' sum= ;
   summiss=sum(.,a) ;
   put 'Sum of missing values only :  ' summiss= ;
   sumzero=sum(0,.,a) ;
   put 'Sum of 0 and missing values : ' sumzero= ;
  * See how the missing value compares to zero ;
   if a<0 then
     put 'Missing is less than 0' ;
   else if a>0 then
     put 'Missing is greater than 0' ;
 run ;
```

In the following log, you can see the results of performing various operations on missing values. You will also notice the NOTE: about missing values being generated. This note warns you that some calculations in your code contain missing values and have, therefore, resulted in missing values. Usually you don't want this to happen, so be aware of this message. Use the (Line):(Column) to locate the places that it occurs so that you can verify that it is OK or else fix it.

```
Addition of missing & non-missing values :  ADD=.
Sum of missing & non-missing values :  SUM=92
Sum of missing values only :  SUMMISS=.
Sum of 0 and missing values :  SUMZERO=0
Missing is less than 0

NOTE: Missing values were generated as a result of performing
an operation on missing values.
Each place is given by: (Number of times) at (Line):(Column).
1 at 77:8     1 at 77:10     1 at 77:12     1 at 81:11
The DATA statement used 0.02 CPU seconds and 1420K.
```

5. Special missing values are handled in a way you may not necessarily expect. It is not the case that if you "do something" with a special missing value, it will be propagated as a special missing value. Consider the following example.

```
data temp;
   missing Z;
   input a;
   b = a + 0;
cards;
7
4
.Z
5
;

proc print ;
run ;
```

In the output you may have expected that the special missing value when added to 0 would result in the same special missing value (.Z). However, it results in a normal missing value (.). Note that the 'Z' shown in the output is actually the missing value '.Z'. SAS does not yet print it as '.Z'.

OBS	A	B
1	7	7
2	4	4
3	z	.
4	5	5

NOTE: Z is a special missing value, which is different from a normal missing value.

Saving resources when the log is long

Why? *When writing a lot of information to the log in an interactive SAS program, you can be slowed down as SAS scrolls the log to display each line as it is written. This is the default behavior, which works well when you don't write much to the log. This tip will tell you how to save time and resources by altering the AUTOSCROLL setting.*

Activating the LOG window (by selecting Log from the Globals menu or simply clicking on the LOG window) and setting AUTOSCROLL to 0 tells SAS not to bother scrolling the LOG window until the DATA step is finished. AUTOSCROLL can be set by using the pull down menus to choose EDIT then OPTIONS then AUTOSCROLL.

The example writes 2000 lines (that is, 2 lines per PUT statement) to the log. The first execution (130 secs) uses the default AUTOSCROLL value, whereas the second execution (27 secs) sets AUTOSCROLL to 0.

```
data _null_ ;
  set sasuser.fitness;
  do i=1 to 1000 ;
    put _all_ ;
  end ;
  stop ;
run ;
NOTE: The DATA statement used 2 minutes 10.33 seconds.

.....  same code but with AUTOSCROLL set to 0 .....
NOTE: The DATA statement used 26.42 seconds.
```

Additional SAS documentation

If you want more information about the tips covered in this section, then try reading the relevant SAS documentation.

These manuals include:

- *SAS Programming Tips: A Guide to Efficient SAS Processing*
- *SAS Companion for the OS/2 Environment, Version 6, First Edition*
- *SAS Companion for the MVS Environment, Version 6, Second Edition*
- *SAS Companion for the Microsoft Windows Environment, Version 6, First Edition*
- *SAS Companion for the Microsoft Windows Environment, Version 6, Second Edition*
- *SAS Software: Abridged Reference, Version 6, First Edition*
- *SAS Language and Procedures: Usage 2, Version 6, First Edition*

Chapter 2
Resource Tips

22 ways to save disk space

Disk space equates to cost. Reducing space means the need for less disk hardware and, therefore, less cost.

1. Use PROC DATASETS, the DIR window or the Libraries window to delete temporary data sets after use.

2. Use the KEEP= or DROP= data set option (or both) to limit the data set to only the variables required. You can also use the KEEP or DROP statement (or both) to do this.

3. Use the WHERE= data set option or WHERE statement to limit the number of observations processed by procedures or DATA steps. Often a WHERE clause can replace a DATA step that contains an IF statement. If you can use WHERE processing, then do.

4. Use _NULL_ as the data set name in the DATA statement when you don't need to create a data set.

5. Use remote library services so that you only need to keep one copy of data on your network.

6. Put temporary data sets on RAM disk (Windows and OS/2), VIO (MVS and CMS) or Hiperspace (MVS). Of course, this requires a lot of spare system memory.

7. Use data set compression (COMPRESS=YES). Be careful because this MAY increase your storage (for example, when you have mostly numeric data). Compression will potentially slightly increase your CPU time used. Compression is best suited for data that has a lot of character values, such as names and addresses.

8. Use views, rather than temporary data sets.

9. Use pipes to compressed data (for operating systems that support pipes). These enable compressed data to be read and written in real time. Please see your operating system companion for more information.

10. Use SQL to merge, summarize, sort, and so on rather than use a combination of procedures and DATA steps with temporary data sets.

11. Keep temporary files on tape, cartridge, optical disk or other high-capacity media.

12. Use the SQL Pass-Through facility to allow SQL to use temporary file space of the server SQL system (which is often a larger complex).

13. Produce a format and store coded values in your data set. The values are decoded using the format.

14. Put your data into something approaching 3rd-normal form; however, this can affect your systems performance.

15. Store your data in the order in which it is usually required. This avoids the need to re-sort data, thereby saving work space. Indexes can be added to avoid re-sorting too.

16. When reading a file into a data set, delete any observation as soon as it is determined that you don't need it as output.

17. Use the LENGTH statement to limit the bytes used to represent a number or character to what is required for the desired precision. You must be careful when doing this for numerics, since the precision can be affected. It is safest only to do so for characters and integer numerics, unless you are sure of what you are doing. See the SAS Advanced Programming course for more information on this.

18. An ideal technique for reducing the space required to store SAS dates is to reduce the length of the variable to 4. You only require 4 bytes of storage, not 8, to store any date.

19. Minimize the data that you keep in your permanent SAS libraries. Ask yourself several questions to determine whether you should keep variables in a data set, or indeed, the data set itself:

■ Do I need this data? (What value is the information that it represents?)

■ Can data within the data set be derived from other information that I have? (For example don't keep month, year and day if you have date.)

■ Is there another copy that I can refer to (for example, data held in DB2)?

■ Is the cost of reproducing the data high? (That is, can I re-run my SAS program to reproduce the data?)

■ Am I likely to need to refer to this data before it is outdated? (Daily data may only be useful for a day.)

■ How much is it costing to keep this data (disk charges, etc.)?

■ Can I tell the system to delete my data when it is of no use? (For example, automatic deletion after 30 days)

■ Can I summarize historical data and delete details if I never again need it?

20. Delete any unused indexes. Make sure that the indexes are not being used by anyone before deleting.

21. Store application code centrally rather than distributing it to users.

22. If the length of numeric ID variables is more than 8 digits (Note: default numeric length is 8), save them as numeric variables, such as account number, Social Security number or employee, student ID (all numbers). This also applies for 8 or fewer digits. For example, a 2 byte number (in MVS) can represent a 5 digit number up to 65,536; and a 6 byte number can represent a 13 digit number up to 1,099,511,627,776 - see your host specific documentation. For example

* Don't use: `length ID $ 16 ;`

* Instead use: `length ID 8 ;` which will save half the space!

How to save space in SAS catalogs

When developing in SAS/AF software, catalogs are not automatically compressed. As you save catalog entries, unused space accumulates. In some cases I have seen, less than half the space used by a catalog is actually needed.

To compress and reuse the space in a catalog, which would otherwise be wasted after doing many compiles, use the REPAIR statement in PROC DATASETS.

This will compress SASUSER.PROFILE.

```
proc datasets library=sasuser ;
   repair profile / mt=cat ;
quit ;
```

10 ways to minimize I/O

I/O, input and output to disk, is the factor that usually slows down SAS programs. Reducing I/O will speed up execution and often reduce costs.

Generally, SAS is I/O intensive, rather than CPU intensive. As the great performance and tuning guru Ken Williams says, "The best I/O is the one you didn't do." Thus, a saving in I/O will improve the performance of your SAS program.

Here are 10 ways to minimize I/O:

1. Use the LENGTH statement to minimize variable lengths, where possible.

2. Use the CLASS statement, where possible, rather than the BY statement, which might require a SORT.

3. Use DROP and KEEP statements to minimize observation length.

4. Only sort when necessary.

5. Read raw data only once, keeping it in permanent data sets if the data is required again.

6. Create multiple data sets in one DATA step if possible.

7. Use the WHERE statement with procedures to avoid using a DATA step and to avoid subsetting in a DATA step.

8. Use the _NULL_ DATA step when you don't need to keep the output.

9. Compress some large SAS data sets, but beware that compression can use more space in some cases, which might actually increase I/O.

10. Develop and test programs on a small subset of the data.

NOTE: The list is not comprehensive, it merely attempts to provide a few ideas for investigation. Not all of the points will always reduce I/O time.

Implementing application data security

2

 The aim is to let permitted users access data via your application but to make it very difficult for anyone to access data without your application. The application should detect who the user is and should provide appropriate data access for them.

Data Set Passwords

From Release 6.07 on, you can put passwords on SAS data sets (as you could in Version 5). This prevents accessing them without specifying the password. This also prevents users from accessing SAS data sets in their own batch jobs (unless they know the password). Passwords can be coded into AF source code so that your application 'knows' the password. AF code can then be distributed without the source code and the source code kept in a secure library. For frames, source code is kept in SCL entries, but executable code is kept in the FRAME entry.

Operating System Security

On MVS you may have RACF or ACF2 to secure your datasets. On PC LANs you can normally protect directories from unauthorized users. On standalone PCs you can often specify a startup password.

Data Encryption

An encryption key (or algorithm) can be used to encode numbers or text and can be kept in a secure data set. It can be read in when compiling the application or can even be built by an algorithm in the code. Different encryption keys can be used for different groupings of information to add another level of security. This means that a 'hacker' would need many encryption keys to access all of the data.

- In SAS Release 6.11 there is also the ENCRYPT data set option, which makes SAS encrypt your data sets.

Other Points

- The user should be exited from SAS when the application ends.

- Close secured files when they have been used. Free FILENAME and LIBNAME allocations when you are finished with them.

- For MVS specify the NOSTAX system option so that the attention key will end the SAS session.

Use indexes with WHERE clauses

Prior to Release 6.08, composite indexes (an index with more than one variable) were fully utilized in a BY clause. However, only the first variable was used in a WHERE clause, and then a sequential pass was made through the data that were returned by using that first variable and the index. In all currently supported releases, this is not the case, though; all variables of a composite index are used.

Be careful that you put first in the WHERE statement the variable whose index you want used. If there are several indexes that you could use, then put the variable whose index would return the least number of observations first in the WHERE clause.

The following example demonstrates that the composite index is only used when we use the first variable of the composite index in the WHERE clause. This makes perfect sense when you think about it.

```
1     proc datasets library=sasuser;
2     modify houses ;
3     index create indx=(style bedrooms) ;
NOTE: Composite index INDX defined.
4     run ;
5     options msglevel=i ; * Show indexes that are used ;
NOTE: The PROCEDURE DATASETS used 0.02 CPU seconds and 1511K.

6     data temp ;
7        set sasuser.houses ;
8           where style='RANCH' ;
INFO: Index INDX selected for WHERE clause optimization.
9     run ;

NOTE: The data set WORK.TEMP has 4 observations and 6 vari-
ables.
NOTE: The DATA statement used 0.02 CPU seconds and 1602K.
10    data temp ;
11       set sasuser.houses ;
12          where bedrooms=3 ;
13    run ;       * Note - No Index was selected for use here ;

NOTE: The data set WORK.TEMP has 4 observations and 6 vari-
ables.
NOTE: The DATA statement used 0.01 CPU seconds and 1602K.
```

Use composite indexes with WHERE clauses

Starting in Release 6.07, the SAS System will take advantage of a composite index when a special form of the WHERE clause is used. The description is in SAS Technical Report P-222, page 21, and is very brief.

The 'special form' is multiple '=' conditions connected with the 'AND' operator.

Assume there is a composite index on, say, variables A, B, and C.

Then "where A = 'x' and B = 'y' and C = 'z'" will take full advantage of the index. The SAS System will concatenate 'x', 'y', and 'z' and look up the concatenated value in the index, thus using all three variables.

Note that the order of the AND conditions is not relevant. "where C = 'z' and A = 'x' and B = 'y'" will work just as well, and "where A = 'x' and B = 'y'" will take advantage of the first two variables in the index.

Furthermore, "where A = 'x' and B = 'y' and C = 'z' and D = 'k'" will use the index for A, B, and C. Then, a secondary filtering will select the "D = 'k'" values. This secondary filtering is not limited to composite indexes.

SAS/GRAPH LINK TO attribute

2

The graphics editor may be used to construct a graph made up of several other graphs, a little like PROC GREPLAY with a template. By using the LINK TO attribute, the graph created can be linked to other graphs. This means that when your graph is referenced at execution time it will be recomposed from the LINK TO graphs. Although this can be a useful technique in some circumstances, there is, of course, a performance overhead.

Useful options for tuning

When tuning your SAS program to make it run more efficiently, it is useful to turn on various information options available in SAS. Remember to turn them off when you finish the tuning and come to run your program, since many options increase the overheads (CPU time, elapsed time, I/Os) of your program.

```
options oplist stats fullstats echoauto source source2 memrpt
mprint stimer ;
```

Option	Description
oplist	Show settings of SAS system options in SAS log
stats	Write performance stats to log
fullstats	Write performance stats in expanded form
echoauto	Show autoexec file in log
source	Show source code in the log
source2	Show included source code in the log
memrpt	Show memory report
mprint	Show statements generated by macro facility
stimer	Maintain and print timing stats (Don't use this with views)

SAS dynamic link libraries under Windows & OS/2

I have used the following technique to improve the response time of online applications.

You can get information on what SAS images SAS loads as you use it. You can then place commonly used images on storage devices that are accessible faster. For example, images that you use frequently could be moved from a network drive to your local hard disk or even to a RAM drive.

Invoking SAS with the -LOADLIST option (*SAS Companion for the Microsoft Windows Environment, Version 6, First Edition*, pg.165) will list images loaded and purged (see example).

```
NOTE: Image purged is Q:\SAS\core\sasexe\SABXINI.DLL
NOTE: Image loaded is Q:\SAS\core\sasexe\SASZAF.DLL
```

Entering the DM command 'cde i' (*SAS Companion for the Microsoft Windows Environment, Version 6, First Edition*, pg. 162) will display a table (see below) showing SAS image usage information. This table is particularly useful in telling you how many times particular images are accessed (Usg column). The table also gives an indication of how your memory is being used (see Total and Deletable Sizes).

```
+--------+-----+---+---+-------+----+----+----+----+----+
|Img Name|ApTyp|Usg|Del|Task ID| Sel|Size|Type|Flag|Pres|
+--------+-----+---+---+-------+----+----+----+----+----+
|SASCBT  |CAPUS|  1|YES|       |3387|ED91|CODE|1D10| YES|
|        |     |   |   |       |092F|0152|DATA|0D31| YES|
|        |     |   |   |       |31FF|0144|CHIP|ODB1| YES|
+--------+-----+---+---+-------+----+----+----+----+----+
|        |     |   |   |       |    |    |    |    |    |

Total      Images=13   Selectors=  81   Size=2727675 bytes
Deletable  Images= 7   Selectors=  27   Size=607837 bytes

Cache: Maximum Entries= 200   Count=  20      Index=  20
```

Once you have decided which modules to move to faster devices, you can use the -PATHDLL option (*SAS Companion for the Microsoft Windows Environment, Version 6, First Edition*, pg. 167) to define the search path that SAS will use to locate SAS images to load.

NOTE: Be very careful when moving DLL files around since some DLL files MUST be kept together or SAS will not start.

2

Additional SAS documentation

If you want more information about the tips covered in this section, then try reading the relevant SAS documentation.

These manuals include:

■ *Tuning SAS Applications in the MVS Environment*

■ *SAS Language and Procedures: Usage 2, Version 6, First Edition*

■ *SAS Companion for the Microsoft Windows Environment, Version 6, First Edition*

Chapter 3
Functions

3

Incrementing and rounding by time intervals

Some coders devote large chunks of code to the task of figuring out which is the last day of the month, whether it is a leap year, etc. That is totally unnecessary if they make use of the INTNX function.

Syntax: INTNX(*interval,from,number*)

This function returns a SAS date, time or datetime value that is incremented a number of time intervals (days, hours, or whatever you specify). See *SAS Language: Reference* for more detailed information about the INTNX function.

The function can be used to set a value to the start of the specified interval by incrementing by 0 time intervals.

```
data _null_ ;
   format date date7. datetime datetime16. time time8. ;
   date=intnx('month','8sep94'd,0) ;
   datetime=intnx('dtday','8sep94:12:34:56'dt,0) ;
   time=intnx('hour','12:34't,0) ;
   put date= / datetime= / time= ;
run ;


DATE=01SEP94
DATETIME=08SEP94:    00:00:00
TIME=12:00:00
NOTE:  The DATA statement used 0.01 CPU seconds and 1473K.
```

One other fine use of INTNX is to get the last day of a month or year -

```
/* SASDAY is a SAS variable containing a SAS date */
/* LASTDAY is the last day of the month of SASDAY */
LASTDAY = INTNX("MONTH",SASDAY,1) - 1;
```

An enhancement to the INTNX function in SAS Release 6.11 is an added argument that causes the function to return a value aligned to either the beginning, middle or end of the interval specified.

INTNX is one of those incredibly useful features that makes SAS stand out from many other languages and that saves you a lot of time and effort.

Various forms for function argument lists

You can specify arguments to functions in various ways. For instance, you can nest functions within functions:

```
sum(mean(x,y,log(z)),a+12,sqrt(total)) ;
```

You can also specify various lists of variables. (Note that the SUM function is merely used as an example.)

sum(a,b,c,d)	Uses all the listed elements.
sum(of a b c d)	Uses all the listed elements.
sum(of x1-x99)	Uses the 99 variables from x1 to x99 (that is, x1, x2, x3, ... x99).
sum(of array(*))	Uses all elements of an array.
sum(of _numeric_)	Uses all numeric variables in the DATA step.
sum(of x—a)	Uses all variables defined in the Program Data Vector in order from x to a.

For more information

See *SAS Language: Reference* - pages 50-51.

Determining which SAS products you have

Determining which SAS products you have can be quite useful in applications devel-opment to make the most of whatever facilities are available. You can check to see if SAS/GRAPH is available. If so, you produce a hi-resolution graph; otherwise, you use the base SAS CHART procedure.

From SAS Release 6.07 onwards, a new DATA step function was released called SYSPROD. This is used to determine if a SAS product is licensed at your site or not.

The function returns 1 if the product is licensed, 0 if it is not, and -1 if it is not a product name.

```
x=sysprod('graph') ;
```

One problem some people have found when using this function on PC platforms - particu-larly Microsoft Windows - is that people have got the product licensed but did not bother to **install** it. SAS/GRAPH is the obvious example. When SAS Institute did the Excel-DDE interface, they had a lot of trouble with this. They updated it to look real nice with lots of graphics entries in frames - but first checked if SAS/GRAPH was licensed - and fell into the trap above.

The way SAS Institute got around it is the following:

```
if sysprod('GRAPH') and cexist('SASHELP.DEVICES') then ...
```

When SAS/GRAPH is installed, the device drivers are also in SASHELP.DEVICES, so this works pretty well, and they have not had any more problems.

Another way to detect the existence of a product is to check for its directory, since in cur-rent releases of SAS each product creates a directory for its files.

Peculiarities of the LENGTH function

You may expect the length of a null character string to be 0, but that is not correct.

SAS Language: Reference states that the length is "an integer representing the position of the right-most non-blank character." *SAS Language: Reference* also states that "if the value of the argument is missing, LENGTH returns a value of 1."

The length of a space (" ") or missing value (" ") is 1, not 0 as you might expect.

```
data _null_ ;
  blank=length(' ') ;
  missing=length('') ;
  normal=length('sas') ;
  put blank= / missing= / normal= ;
run ;
BLANK=1
MISSING=1
NORMAL=3
NOTE: The DATA statement used 0.01 CPU seconds and 1351K.
```

Using the TRIM function makes no difference to the length, since length reports the position of the "right-most non-blank character".

```
data _null_ ;
  blank=length(trim(' ')) ;
  missing=length(trim('')) ;
  normal=length(trim('sas')) ;
  put blank= / missing= / normal= ;
run ;
BLANK=1
MISSING=1
NORMAL=3
NOTE: The DATA statement used 0.01 CPU seconds and 1351K.
```

If you try the LENGTH function on numbers, then you will have 12 returned by default. You even get 12 returned if the numeric variable had a missing value. The reason for this is that the format BEST12. is used when converting the numbers to characters for use with the LENGTH function. The numbers are right justified and, therefore, show as having a length of 12.

```
data _null_ ;
   length a 4 ;
   length b 6 ;
   length c 8 ;
   a=-123.3;
   b=9999999999;
   len_a=length(a) ;
   len_b=length(b) ;
   len_c=length(c) ;
   put len_a= / len_b= / len_c= ;
run ;
NOTE: Numeric values have been converted to character
values at the places given by: (Line):(Column).
65:16    66:16    67:16
NOTE: Variable C is uninitialized.
LEN_A=12
LEN_B=12
LEN_C=12
NOTE: The DATA statement used 0.01 CPU seconds and 1351K.
```

For more information

See *SAS Language: Reference*, page 566.

Random numbers are not always random

You may expect random numbers to always be random, but that is not always the case.

The UNIFORM function (same as RANUNI) of base SAS produces a uniform series of random numbers between 0 and 1. A seed is specified to start the series off - if the seed is <=0 then the system time is used. For each seed you will always get the same sequence of "random" numbers. This means that they are repeatable, and therefore in one sense NOT random.

So if you use a static seed (such as 1 in my example below) you can produce a repeatable sequence of numbers.

This applies to the other SAS random functions also (RANTRI, RANPOI, and so on.).

```
* Make 100 random numbers with a seed of 1 ;
data a ;
  do i=1 to 100 ;
    x=uniform(1) ;
    output ;
  end ;
run ;
```

```
NOTE: The data set WORK.A has 100 observations and 2 vari-
ables.
NOTE: The DATA statement used 0.01 CPU seconds and 1442K.
```

```
* Make another 100 random numbers with the same seed ;
data b ;
  do i=1 to 100 ;
    x=uniform(1) ;
    output ;
  end ;
run ;
```

```
NOTE: The data set WORK.B has 100 observations and 2 vari-
ables.
NOTE: The DATA statement used 0.01 CPU seconds and 1442K.
```

```
* Compare the 2 datasets of random numbers ;
proc compare data=a compare=b ;
  var x ;
run ;
```

```
NOTE: The PROCEDURE COMPARE used 0.02 CPU seconds and 2114K.
```

This output shows that all the observations are the same.

Output: from Proc Compare

```
                         The SAS System                    3
                            07:13 Wednesday, December 21, 1994


                         COMPARE Procedure
                    Comparison of WORK.A with WORK.B
                          (Method=EXACT)


                        Observation Summary

                   Observation      Base  Compare

                   First Obs          1        1
                   Last  Obs        100      100

Number of Observations in Common: 100.
Total Number of Observations Read from WORK.A: 100.
Total Number of Observations Read from WORK.B: 100.


Number of Observations with Some Compared Variables Unequal: 0.
Number of Observations with All Compared Variables Equal: 100.


NOTE: No unequal values were found. All values compared are exactly
      equal.
```

Minimum/Maximum arithmetic operators

These operators are executed from right to left, like the leading minus sign and unlike virtually all the other operators. This leads to the amazing result that

```
-3 >< -3
```

is positive three when it "obviously" should be negative three!

The reason that SAS returns positive 3 is that the expression is treated as being:

```
- (3 >< -3)
```

```
data _null_ ;
  x=-3><-3 ;
  put x= ;
run ;
X=3
NOTE: The DATA statement used 0.01 CPU seconds and 1410K.
```

There are operators that can be used for returning minimum and maximum in arithmetic expressions. Minimum uses the operator ><, and maximum uses <>.

If you wanted to assign the maximum of two variables X and Y to a third variable Z, then rather than coding

```
if x>y then
  z=x ;
else
  z=y ;
```

you could code the following. Note that the problem with negative numbers mentioned above does not occur in this code since the problem only occurs when there is a literal as the first argument and both numbers are negative. Having the first argument as a variable avoids the problem.

```
z=x<>y ;
```

Min/Max Confusion

In SAS arithmetic >< means minimum.

In SAS PROC SQL (and standard SQL) <> means not-equal.

In WHERE clauses <> also means not-equal.

```
      proc print data=sasuser.crime ;
      where staten<>'Alaska' ; run ;
NOTE: The "<>" operator is interpreted as "not equals".

NOTE: The PROCEDURE PRINT used 0.02 CPU seconds and 1503K.
```

It may be advisable to use the MAX and MIN functions, which would seem to be more self documenting to the casual reader. These functions work the same in SAS arithmetic and in SQL. You can have 2 or more arguments to these functions as shown in the following example:

```
z = MIN(x,y,z);
```

For more information

See *SAS Language: Reference*, page 127.

Getting the remainder of a division

The MOD function returns negative values when the first argument is negative. This could be thought to be "mathematically incorrect".

```
data _null_ ;
   x=mod(-3, 2) ; put 'mod(-3, 2)=' x ;
   x=mod(-3,-2) ; put 'mod(-3,-2)=' x ;
   x=mod( 3, 2) ; put 'mod( 3, 2)=' x ;
   x=mod( 3,-2) ; put 'mod( 3,-2)=' x ;
run ;


mod(-3, 2)=-1
mod(-3,-2)=-1
mod( 3, 2)=1
mod( 3,-2)=1
NOTE: The DATA statement used 0.01 CPU seconds and 1398K.
```

The "trap" with the MOD function is not that it produces mathematically incorrect results but that the function name (MOD) implies *modulo* or *clock* arithmetic.

It is (and has always been) simply the "remainder" function.

It represents (arg1 - (int(arg1/arg2) * arg2)).

"The MOD function returns the remainder when the integer quotient of argument-1 divided by argument-2 is calculated." (*SAS Language: Reference*, p. 571) The output from the code shown in the previous log follows:

arg-1	arg-2	integer quotient= int(arg1/arg2)	remainder
-3	2	-1	-1
-3	-2	1	-1
3	2	1	1
3	-2	-1	1

As in other cases throughout SAS (For example, LAG), MOD does exactly what it is designed to do but not what many of us would expect given its name. Read the manual carefully, and you will find that it behaves as it is documented.

For more information

See *SAS Language: Reference*, page 571.

Additional SAS documentation

If you want more information about the tips covered in this section, then try reading the relevant SAS documentation.

These manuals include:

- *SAS Language and Procedures: Usage 2, Version 6, First Edition*
- *SAS Language: Reference, Version 6, First Edition*

Chapter 4
DATA Step

4

4

How to rearrange variables in a data set

To rearrange the order of variables in your SAS data set you can use the RETAIN statement before the SET statement.

Alternatively, you can use a KEEP statement before the SET statement. In fact any code which refers to variables in the order which you require, before the SET statement, causes the variables to appear in that order in the Program Data Vector.

```
data new ;
   retain this that theother ;
   set old ;
run ;
```

Using pattern matching in WHERE clauses

Pattern matching provides a lot more flexibility in specifying criteria for selecting data using a WHERE clause.

The LIKE operator of the WHERE clause enables you to use pattern matching in DATA and PROC steps.

■ An underscore (_) in a pattern will match any character in that position.

■ A percent sign (%) in a pattern will match any number of characters in that position.

■ A colon modifier (For example =:) used at the end of any comparison operator lets you match the first characters of the longer value with those of the shorter value.

■ The contains operator (and ?) matches strings that include the character string after the operator.

■ The sounds-like operator (*) can be used to match slight spelling variations - refer to the manual and try it out.

All of the following examples would match `name='Phil Mason'`:

```
where name=:'Ph' ;
where name like 'P_il M_s_n' ;
where name like '%son' ;
where name contains 'il' ;
where name ? 'hil' ;
where name=*'PFil Mason' ;
```

For more information

Refer to *SAS Language: Reference,* pages 501-502 and 519 for explanations of these and other WHERE clause operators

Conditionally generating code with CALL EXECUTE

Sometimes, depending on data from some source, you might want to conditionally generate SAS code from a SAS program. CALL EXECUTE is an efficient way to do this.

You can use CALL EXECUTE to set up SAS code that will be executed after a DATA step ends. This is similar to the traditional method of putting statements out to a temporary file and then including them into the SAS stream using %INCLUDE.

This takes care of about 90% of the reasons that most people would like to use %IF macro statements in open code, which of course cannot be done since %IF statements only work inside a macro.

Log: Example using a DATA step

```
data _null_ ;
   call execute('data y;set sasuser.crime;run;');
run;

NOTE: The DATA statement used 0.01 CPU seconds and 1452K.

NOTE: CALL EXECUTE generated line.
   +data y;set sasuser.crime;run;

NOTE: The data set WORK.Y has 50 observations and 9 variables.
NOTE: The DATA statement used 0.01 CPU seconds and 1540K.
```

Log: Example using macros

```
%macro x;
   %put Line 1 ;
   %put Line 2 ;
%mend x;

%macro y;
   %put Line 3 ;
   %put Line 4 ;
%mend y;

data _null_ ;
   call execute('%x %y %x %y');
run;
```

```
Line 1
Line 2
Line 3
Line 4
Line 1
Line 2
Line 3
Line 4
NOTE: The DATA statement used 0.01 CPU seconds and 1452K.

NOTE: CALL EXECUTE generated line.
```

DDE: writing data to Lotus 123

Often users require that data from SAS is put into another product which they are familiar with so that they can use the data. Spreadsheets are a common destination, and DDE enables data to be quickly and easily put into spreadsheets.

Dynamic Data Exchange (DDE) enables applications to send and receive data between one another. There are two main steps to using DDE to write values to an application from SAS:

1. Define the fileref. It is made up of the keyword FILENAME, fileref keyword DDE, and then the DDE triplet. The DDE triplet is made up of the application name, topic and item.

   app. name   This is the name of the program executing, without its extension. For example, Lotus 123 executes 123w.exe, so the application name is 123w.

   | A vertical bar separates application and topic.

   topic   This is the file name being used by the application. If it's not in the current path, then it needs a full specification.

   !   An exclamation mark separates the Topic and Item.

   item   This defines the range that the DDE will operate on.

2. Write out the data.

   Merely write out your data to the range. If you write more rows or columns than are in your range, then they will not appear in the spreadsheet. The DDE link is like a window into the spreadsheet, only letting you see what is in the window.

```
* Define FILEREF for DDE
  application = 123w.exe (Lotus 123 for Windows)
  topic/file  = test.wk4 in current working directory of lotus 123
  item/range  = Sheet A, position A1 to B2 ;

filename lotus dde '123w|test.wk4!a:a1..a:b2' notab ;

* Write values directly to spreadsheet via DDE ;
data _null_ ;
  retain '09'x ;        *** Define a tab character ;
  file lotus ;          *** Directs output to spreadsheet via DDE link ;
  put 'Name:'    tab
      'Rod Krishock' tab /
      'Address:'  tab
      'Adelaide'  ;
run ;

NOTE: The file LOTUS is:
      FILENAME=123w|test.wk4!a:a1..a:b2,
```

```
   RECFM=V,LRECL=256

NOTE: 2 records were written to the file LOTUS.
      The minimum record length was 18.
      The maximum record length was 29.
NOTE: The DATA statement used 0.71 seconds.
```

4

DDE: writing to Microsoft Word

Writing data from SAS to Microsoft Word requires a slightly different DDE triplet than writing to a spreadsheet. The triplet is made up of the program name, document name and bookmark name. A bookmark can be inserted into MS Word using the Edit menu. Bookmarks can then be referred to by defining a FILEREF for each one.

This example uses 2 bookmarks defined in doc1.doc. The first is positioned so that a name can be inserted. The second is positioned in the text of a letter so that some text can be inserted.

```
filename name dde 'WinWord|doc1.doc!name' notab ; *** First
bookmark ;
filename problem dde 'WinWord|doc1.doc!problem' notab ; ***
Second bookmark ;

data _null_ ;
   file name ;
   put 'Rod Krishock' ;
   file problem ;
   put 'stay in a cheap hotel' ;
run ;

NOTE: The file NAME is:
      FILENAME=WinWord|doc1.doc!name,
      RECFM=V,LRECL=256

NOTE: The file PROBLEM is:
      FILENAME=WinWord|doc1.doc!problem,
      RECFM=V,LRECL=256

NOTE: 1 record was written to the file NAME.
      The minimum record length was 12.
      The maximum record length was 12.
NOTE: 1 record was written to the file PROBLEM.
      The minimum record length was 21.
      The maximum record length was 21.
NOTE: The DATA statement used 0.93 seconds.
```

DDE: operating other programs from SAS

Using DDE, SAS is able to control other programs by issuing recognizable commands to them. The commands that are used depend on the application being controlled. A simple way to find out which commands to use is to turn on the application's macro recorder, do something, and then edit the macro recorded to see what the commands are.

Steps to control applications "remotely" from SAS.

1. Work out what commands to use, either with the manual or the macro recorder.

2. Allocate the fileref. Remember to use the applications program name and the word SYS-TEM separated by a vertical bar.

3. Write commands to the fileref. Commands should be contained within square brackets.

Following are two examples, one controlling Lotus 123 and the other Microsoft Word.

Example I

```
    *** Program name is 123w.exe ;
filename lotus dde '123w|system' notab ;
data _null_ ;
  file lotus ;
  *** Create a new chart ;
  put '[run({CHART-NEW A:A1..A:F14})]' ;
  put '[run({SELECT "CHART 1";;"CHART"})]' ; *** Select it ;
  *** Set the X range ;
  put '[run({CHART-RANGE "X";A:A1..A:A4;"Line";"NO"})]' ;
  * Set the Y range and plot a bar chart ;
  put '[run({CHART-RANGE "A";A:B1..A:B4;"Bar";"NO"}dd)]' ;
run ;


NOTE: The file LOTUS is:
      FILENAME=123w|system,
      RECFM=V,LRECL=256


NOTE: 4 records were written to the file LOTUS.
      The minimum record length was 30.
      The maximum record length was 48.
NOTE: The DATA statement used 1.37 seconds.
```

Example 2

```
    *** Program name is Winword.exe ;
filename word dde 'winword|system' notab ;
data _null_ ;
  file word ;
  *** Open a file called phill.doc ;
  put '[FileOpen .Name = "phill.DOC"]' ;
  put '[macro1]' ; *** Execute a macro called macro1 ;
run ;
```

```
NOTE: The file WORD is:
      FILENAME=WinWord|system,
      RECFM=V,LRECL=256

NOTE: 1 record was written to the file WORD.
      The minimum record length was 30.
      The maximum record length was 30.
NOTE: The DATA statement used 3.62 seconds.
```

DDE: make sure numbers are numeric

Sometimes when writing out data using DDE, you might find that you can't do calculations on the numbers that you have written to your spreadsheet or database. This is because the numbers have been written out as character values, rather than numbers.

When using DDE to write numbers to a spreadsheet/database, they can sometimes be inadvertently read in as character values. This can happen if you use a variable to hold your tab character since a space is written after a variable is output. To get around this, position the column pointer over the space that was written (see example).

4

```
filename lotus dde '123w|test.wk4!a:a1..a:b3' notab ;

* Writing numeric values directly to spreadsheet via DDE ;
data _null_ ;
  retain tab '09'x ; ** Define a tab character ;
  file lotus ; ** Directs output to spreadsheet via DDE link ;
 * In Lotus: 1 is numeric, but 2 is character due to implicit
space after variable TAB ;
 *           3 & 4 are numeric, since implicit space is over-
written ;
 *           5 & 6 are numeric since there is no implicit
space, due to constant being used ;
  put '1'     tab
      '2'     /
      '3'     tab +(-1)
      '4'     /
      '5'     '09'x
      '6'     ;
run ;

NOTE: The file LOTUS is:
      FILENAME=123w|test.wk4!a:a1..a:b3,
      RECFM=V,LRECL=256

NOTE: 3 records were written to the file LOTUS.
      The minimum record length was 3.
      The maximum record length was 4.
NOTE: The DATA statement used 0.66 seconds.
```

DDE: using more advanced commands

DDE system commands are issued by setting up a fileref to point to an application, as in the example below. The commands can then be sent to the application by writing to the fileref. When issuing commands to the application, the SYSITEMS system command can be used to discover what commands the program supports. These commands offer a greater level of interaction between SAS and the other program. Using the SYSITEMS command on Lotus 123, I discovered that it supports six commands (see example below), whereas Microsoft Word 6 supports only three of those commands.

Lotus 123

SysItems   returns commands available for server (see example below).

Topics   returns topics.

Formats   returns file formats handled by server (for example, RTF, Text, WK3, etc.).

RangeNames   returns name of range and its specification (for example, Sales A:C4..A:E8).

Selection   Returns name of data file and range selected (for example, Untitled A:A1..A:C3).

Status   returns status of server (for example, Ready).

```
** Define the sysitems topic to find which commands are sup-
ported
    by the application for DDE ;
filename lotus dde '123w|system!sysitems' notab ;

data _null_ ;
   length cmd $ 40 ; * Otherwise first command read in sets
maximum length ;
   infile lotus pad dsd dlm='09'x ; * One tab delimited record
is returned ;
   input cmd $ @@ ;
   put cmd ;
run ;

NOTE: The infile LOTUS is:
      FILENAME=123w|system!sysitems,
      RECFM=V,LRECL=256
```

```
SysItems
Topics
Formats
RangeNames
Selection
Status
NOTE: 1 record was read from the infile LOTUS.
      The minimum record length was 51.
      The maximum record length was 51.
NOTE: SAS went to a new line when INPUT statement reached past
the end of a line.
NOTE: The DATA statement used 0.82 seconds.
```

Microsoft Word

```
** Define the sysitems topic to find which commands are sup-
ported
   by the application for DDE ;
filename word dde 'winword|system!sysitems' notab ;

data _null_ ;
  infile word pad dsd dlm='09'x ; * One tab separated record
is returned ;
  input cmd $ @@ ;
  put cmd ;
run ;

NOTE: The infile WORD is:
      FILENAME=winword|system!sysitems,
      RECFM=V,LRECL=256

SYSITEMS
TOPICS
FORMATS
NOTE: 1 record was read from the infile WORD.
      The minimum record length was 23.
      The maximum record length was 23.
NOTE: SAS went to a new line when INPUT statement reached past
the end of a line.
NOTE: The DATA statement used 0.81 seconds.
```

Introduction to using arrays

This brief tutorial is intended for those who know SAS but have not used arrays before. If you know SAS arrays well, then please ignore this. If you would like to use arrays in SAS and haven't before, then you might like to read this.

In SAS an array is merely a convenient way of temporarily referring to a group of variables. An array is not a data structure, it only exists in the current DATA step.

Log: Defining and referencing arrays

```
data spree ;
   * use the standard SAS sample dataset for this example ;
   set sasuser.crime(obs=1) ; * only read in the first
observation ;
   array crimes(7) murder rape robbery assault burglary lar-
ceny auto ;
   * the first element of the array is the variable murder ;
   put staten 'murder: ' crimes(1) / ;
   * the last element of the array is the variable auto ;
   put staten 'auto: ' crimes(7) / ;
   * we can go through each element in the array using a loop ;
   do i=1 to 7 ;
      put crimes(i) ;
   end ;
   * we can assign values to variables using arrays ;
   do i=1 to 7 ;
      if crimes(i)=. then
         crimes(i)=0 ;
   end ;
run ;
Alabama Murder: 14.2

Alabama Auto: 280.7

14.2
25.2
96.8
278.3
1135.5
1881.9
280.7
NOTE: The data set WORK.SPREE has 1 observations and 10 vari-
ables.
NOTE: The DATA statement used 0.02 CPU seconds and 1663K.
```

Defining number of array elements

You can either specify the number of elements or you can specify an asterisk to tell SAS to count the variables.

```
* can use this syntax ;
  ARRAY SCORES(3) ONE TWO THREE ;

* or can use this syntax ;
  ARRAY SCORES(*) ONE TWO THREE ;
```

Defining multi-dimensional arrays

A two-dimensional array is like a table of variables with rows and columns. However, you can define any number of dimensions. Just define the number of variables in each dimension and separate the dimensions by commas.

```
ARRAY table(2,2) row1col1 row1col2 row2col1 row2col2 ;
ARRAY test(2,9) name1-name9 score1-score9 ;
```

Determining the number of array elements

Use the DIM function to return the number of elements in a single-dimensional array. Or use DIMn to return the number of elements in the nth dimension of a multi-dimensional array. The function returns the number of elements, whether each element has been initialized with a value or not.

```
* This would return 3 ;
  num_elem=dim(scores) ;
* This would return 9 - see array def. above ;
  num2=dim2(test) ;
```

Setting bounds

Usually the elements of an array are numbered 1 to n, but you can specify how they will be numbered by specifying $x:y$ for each dimension, where x is the number to start with and y is the number to go to.

```
* Refer to element number 31 ;
  ARRAY adults(18:70) age18-age70 ;
  put '31 year old ' adults(31) ;
```

Finding the bounds

Use the LBOUND function to find the lower bound of an array and HBOUND to find the upper bound. For multi-dimensional arrays use LBOUND*n* and HBOUND*n*, in the same way as you use DIM*n*.

```
* Loop through each element of array ;
  do i=lbound(adults) to hbound(adults) ;
    put adults(i) ;
  end ;
```

Setting initial values

You can set initial values for the array elements (for the variables) when you define the array. For example, the first element of the following array is test(1), which is the variable ONE and has a value of 101.

```
array test(2) one two (101 102) ;
```

Temporary arrays

When you only need the variables used in the array for the duration of the DATA step, then you can use a temporary array which defines variables for you to use with the array.

```
* defines array temp and assigns values ;
  array temp(4) _temporary_ (1 2 3 4) ;
```

Adding variables with similar names

Sometimes you may have groups of variables whose names start with the same characters. These can be added (or some other operation can be done) by putting the variables into an array and then using a DO loop to handle each variable as an element of the array.

For example, all variables that describe international phone calls begin with IDD and then have a suffix describing the country the call goes to.

```
      data _null_ ;
    * Sample data ;
      iddusa=10 ;
      iddaus=33 ;
      iddtai=44 ;
      idduk=99 ;
      iddbel=1 ;
      iddcan=11 ;
    * Define array to hold all the IDD variables ;
      array idd(*) idd: ;
    * Initialise total to 0 ;
      total=0 ;
    * Add them up ;
      do i=1 to dim(idd) ;
         total+idd(i) ;
      end ;
    * Calculate average ;
      avg=total/dim(idd) ;
      put _all_ ;
    run ;
```

```
      IDDUSA=10 IDDAUS=33 IDDTAI=44 IDDUK=99 IDDBEL=1 IDDCAN=11
      TOTAL=198 I=7
      AVG=33 _ERROR_=0 _N_=1
```

Inputting data using text value positioning

There are various ways of positioning the pointer for reading in data using the INPUT statement. One of the ways is to use INPUT @'*text*'. This searches the input line for "*text*" and positions the pointer directly after it. This allows data following the "*text*" to be read by SAS. This could be used to read CPU times from the SAS log, for example.

In the following example, I read a SAS log from one of my SAS jobs. Note that the filename SASLOG is not a special automatic fileref but one that I have assigned to a file in which I have stored a previous SAS log.

```
       data logstats ;
          infile saslog ;
          input @'used' duration 6.2 ;
       run ;

       proc print ;
```

OBS	DURATION
1	0.05
2	2.72
3	6.74
4	69.09
5	2.74
6	3.03
7	13.10
8	12.29
9	109.70

For more information

See *SAS Language: Reference*, pages 160-171 and 397.

Reading unaligned data that require informats

With list input, SAS scans the data line for the fields specified in the INPUT state-ment. Fields don't have to be aligned, but they must be separated by at least one space. Format modifiers provide more flexibility in reading data in this way.

Syntax

INPUT *<pointer-control> variable <format-modifier> <informat.> <@!@@>* ;

Format-modifiers

  &   The ampersand allows character values to have single embedded blanks. The field is read until either 2 consecutive blanks or an end-of-line is reached.

  :   The colon allows an informat to be used to read data in. The colon is useful for trun-cating values when the field is longer than the informat specifies. You must put an informat after the colon.

  ~   The tilde, when used in conjunction with the DSD INFILE option, keeps quotes rather than stripping them off (as is the default).

```
data test ;
   infile datalines dsd ;
   input name     :  $20.
         title    ~  $20.
         address  &  $30. ;
   datalines ;
"Phil Mason","SAS Tips guy",Melbourne - Australia
"Mark Bodt","Frame supremo",Auckland - New Zealand
;
proc print ; run ;
```

```
OBS        NAME          TITLE              ADDRESS


 1     Phil Mason    "SAS Tips guy"     Melbourne - Australia
 2     Mark Bodt     "Frame supremo"    Auckland - New
Zealand
```

Do-it-yourself log messages

Entering code such as this ...

```
data _null_;
  put 'NOTE: this is a note';
  put 'WARNING: this is a warning';
  put 'ERROR: this is an error';
run;
```

causes the SAS log to highlight these messages in exactly the same way it highlights its own ERROR messages. What appears to be happening is that SAS examines the first word that is sent to the log and if it is ERROR:, it highlights it. This works in MVS, Windows and other versions I have tried (in fact, it probably works under all versions and platforms). Under MVS overprinting is used for highlighting, whereas in GUI environments colors are used.

In a display manager session under OS/2, the NOTE statement came back with black print, the WARNING with yellow, and the ERROR statement came back red, all just as though they had been issued by the SAS System itself.

NOTE: the keywords must be entered in uppercase, or it will not work - for example, ERROR not error.

I have not been able to find this in any of the manuals or SAS Notes anywhere. It appears to be an undocumented feature and potentially quite a handy one.

Use _NULL_ DATA steps when not creating data sets

Use a _NULL_ DATA step when you need to do DATA step processing but do not need to create a data set. This avoids the overheads (for example I/O, disk space) involved in creating a data set. If you don't need to refer to the data set again, then don't create it.

Be aware that using the DATA statement with no argument will create a default data set called DATA1, DATA2, and so on. Using DATA _NULL_ does not create a data set.

```
data ;
  x=1 ;
run ;

NOTE: The data set WORK.DATA1 has 1 observations and 1 vari-
ables.
NOTE: The DATA statement used 0.01 CPU seconds and 1426K.

data _null_ ;
  x=1 ;
run ;

NOTE: The DATA statement used 0.01 CPU seconds and 1426K.
```

Determining the number of observations in a data set

The NOBS argument in the SET statement assigns the number of observations in the SAS data set to a variable.

Views

The NOBS= option returns 2**31–1 if the data set being read is a view. This makes it very easy to fill up a disk by accident.

```
DATA a_view / view=a_view ;
   set saslib.xpose ;
Run ;

NOTE: DATA STEP view saved on file WORK.A_VIEW.
NOTE: The original source statements cannot be retrieved from
a stored DATA STEP
different release of the SAS system or under a different oper-
ating system.
Please be sure to save the source statements for this DATA
STEP view.
NOTE: The DATA statement used 0.03 CPU seconds.

        DATA _null_ ;
          if 0 then
            set a_view nobs=nobs ;
          put "For a View: " nobs= ;
          stop ;
        Run ;

For a View: NOBS=2147483647
NOTE: The view WORK.A_VIEW.VIEW used 0.01 CPU seconds.
NOTE: The DATA statement used 0.02 CPU seconds.

        DATA temp ;
          if 0 then
            set saslib.xpose nobs=nobs ;
          put "For a Disk dataset: " nobs= ;
          stop ;
        Run ;

For a Disk dataset: NOBS=49
NOTE: The data set WORK.TEMP has 0 observations and 17 vari-
ables.
NOTE: The DATA statement used 0.02 CPU seconds.
```

Note that we used `if 0 then ...` in the code above. This is a useful technique when you do not want a statement to execute. Since NOBS= is set at compile time, its value will be set even though the SET statement is not executed.

OBS and FIRSTOBS

NOBS is unrelated to the OBS= argument and the FIRSTOBS= argument and, therefore, is ignored. Also, WHERE clauses and deleted records are not taken into account. So if you use these parameters to limit the number of observations that your DATA step is processing, the NOBS parameter will still return the total number of observations, including observations that you do not process. Deleted observations, which have been flagged but not removed, are also included in the NOBS count.

```
DATA temp ;
  if 0 then
  set saslib.xpose(firstobs=20 obs=25) nobs=nobs ;
  put "With firstobs & obs: " nobs= ;
  stop ;
Run ;


With firstobs & obs: NOBS=49
NOTE: The data set WORK.TEMP has 0 observations and 17 vari-
ables.
NOTE: The DATA statement used 0.03 CPU seconds.

DATA temp ;
  if 0 then
  set saslib.xpose nobs=nobs ;
  put "WithOUT firstobs & obs: " nobs= ;
  stop ;
Run ;


WithOUT firstobs & obs: NOBS=49
NOTE: The data set WORK.TEMP has 0 observations and 17 vari-
ables.
NOTE: The DATA statement used 0.02 CPU seconds.
```

Tape data sets

On mainframe tape data sets, the number of observations in the data set is not stored in the descriptor portion of the SAS data set (which is at the beginning of the data set, of course) because SAS cannot possibly know when it's beginning to write the tape data set how many observations it will write. For disk data sets, SAS just goes back to the descriptor portion and writes the number of observations into the correct slot once the data set is finished. It's fairly easy to see why this isn't a feature with tape data sets.

You can use the TAPE engine to have sequential data sets stored on disk. In this case the number of observations is also not available.

```
LIBNAME v9305 V606SEQ ;

NOTE: Libref V9305 was successfully assigned as follows:
      Engine:          V606SEQ
      Physical Name: IVXXX.REQ3339.CARTVX2.SAS9305

DATA temp ;
  if 0 then
    set v9305.ServBill nobs=nobs ;
  put nobs= ;
  stop ;
Run ;


NOBS=2147483647
NOTE: The data set WORK.TEMP has 0 observations and 3 vari-
ables.
NOTE: The DATA statement used 0.03 CPU seconds.
```

NOBS available prior to Set

The number of observations in a dataset can be obtained using the NOBS keyword in the SET statement. The variable that you specify to hold the number of observations is set at compile time, so you can access it at run time prior to the SET statement.

You can get the number of observations and store it in a macro variable without reading observations in. This could be useful if you wanted to conditionally run code depending on whether you had data available or not.

```
* code to test if a data set has any obs. ;
data _null_ ;
  if 0 then set work.ytd point=_n_ nobs=count ;
  call symput('numobs',left(put(count,8.))) ; stop ;
run;
```

```
%macro reports ;
%if &numobs =0
%then %do ;
data _null_ ;
   file ft20f001 ;
   %title ;
   put ////
      @10 "NO records were selected using the statement " //
      @15 "&where" //
      @10 "for any month from &start to &end" //
      @10 'THIS RUN HAS COMPLETED SUCCESSFULLY.' ;
run ;
%end ;
%else
   %do ;
* generate graph of costs vs cycle;
proc chart data=work.ytd ;
   by finyear ; vbar pcycle / type=sum sumvar=cost discrete;
format pcycle $2. ; run;
   %end ;
%mend ;

%reports;
```

Creating views from a DATA step

A type of view made available in SAS Release 6.07 onwards is the DATA step view. This is kind of a compiled DATA step that is stored away and is able to run at a later time. It can be used anywhere a data set can be used, which means that complicated DATA steps can be written and stored once and can be used over and over for reporting even as the data changes.

For example, if you had a log file that came to you each month in the form of a large flat file (or CSV, etc.) then you could set up a view to read the records in. This view could then be used in various PROC steps and other DATA steps to analyze and report on the data.

In this example we read in a member that has JCL and SAS code in it. We only keep the lines of JCL in our data set, and make a variable for the account number (if it is there). The print step then only prints the line with the account number.

```
            filename x 'XXXGI.REQ3300.CNTL(SQL)' ;
            data sasuser.readx / view=sasuser.readx ;
            infile x ;
            input line $80. ;
            if index(line,'//') ; * keep jcl lines ;
            acc=index(line,' JOB ')+5 ;
            if acc>5 then
            account=scan(substr(line,acc),1,"'") ;
            run ;

NOTE: DATA STEP view saved on file SASUSER.READX.
NOTE: The original source statements cannot be retrieved from
a stored
DATA STEP view nor will a stored DATA STEP view run under a
different release of the SAS system or under a different oper-
ating system.
Please be sure to save the source statements for this DATA
STEP    view.
NOTE: The DATA statement used 0.01 CPU seconds and 1985K.
            proc print ;
            where account>'' ;
            run ;

NOTE: The infile X is:
Dsname=XXXGI.REQ3300.CNTL(SQL),
Unit=3380,Volume=D00106,Disp=SHR,Blksize=23440,
Lrecl=80,Recfm=FB
NOTE: 45 records were read from the infile X.
NOTE: The view SASUSER.READX.VIEW used 0.02 CPU seconds and
2066K.
NOTE: The PROCEDURE PRINT used 0.01 CPU seconds and 2066K.
```

```
OBS                                  LINE
1        //XXMSPM00 JOB 'XXXGI002','A_3300 (PM9992306)',CLASS=V,

OBS    ACC    ACCOUNT

 1      16    XXXGI002
```

Another excellent use of DATA step views is to improve the performance of pre-processing DATA steps, for example:

```
data work.temp;
set work.large;
if variable >=0 then flag=1;
else flag=0; run;
proc freq data=work.temp;
table flag; run;
```

The previous code requires three I/O's per observation (a read/write by the DATA step and a read by PROC FREQ). Changing WORK.TEMP to a view as shown below, reduces the I/O's to one read, as the DATA step passes the modified observation directly to PROC FREQ. (Adding the KEEP statement reduces the data vector.)

```
data work.temp / VIEW=WORK.TEMP;
  KEEP FLAG;
  set work.large;
  if variable >=0 then flag=1;
                  else flag=0;
run;
proc freq data=work.temp;
  table flag; run;
```

Also, with the original code a work file of a greater size than the original data is required. However, this is not the case using a view, as the modified observations are not kept. The work file only needs to be big enough to hold the compiled view.

Of course, if the view is required frequently, the extra processing cost may out weigh the savings. However, for one-off queries the savings can be very significant.

For more information

DATA step views are covered in *SAS Technical Report P-222: Changes and Enhancements to Base SAS Software, Release 6.07.*

Use the DATA step debugger

This was undocumented but available in some earlier releases of SAS. The debugger is now production in Releases 6.11 and 6.08 (TS430) for MVS/CMS/VMS.

It operates in much the same way as the SCL debugger of SAS/AF, which has been available for a long time. It can be used to step through your DATA step, executing a line at a time. At any stage you can examine the values of variables. You can set break points and run the DATA step until the code gets to your breakpoint.

To invoke the DATA step debugger, simply put / DEBUG in your DATA statement (see example below).

4

Screen Shot

```
+DEBUGGER SOURCE-------------------------------+
! Command ===>                                 !
!                                              !
!    1 data x / debug ;                        !
!    2 set sasuser.crime ;                     !
!    3 a+1*_n_ ;                               !
!    4 run ;                                    !
!                                              !
!                                              !
+----------------------------------------------+
! 3      a+1*_n_ ;                             !
+DEBUGGER LOG----------------------------------+
! Command ===>                                 !
!                                              !
! DATA STEP source level DEBUGGER.             !
! For SAS INSTITUTE INTERNAL use only.         !
!                                              !
!                                              !
!                                              !
!                                              !
!                                              !
!----------------------------------------------!
! >                                            !
+-------------------------------R----------+
```

Here are some of the debugger commands. In the following commands I use l to separate alternate parameters.

Commands

Break line-number	Suspends program execution at an executable statement.
DEScribe arg-list I _all_	Displays the attributes of variable(s).
ENTER command-list	Assigns one or more debugger commands to the Enter key.
Examine arg-list I _all_	Displays the value of one or more variables.
Go line-num I label	Starts or resumes execution of the DATA step.
JUMP line-num	Acts like a GOTO.
List B I W I _all_	Displays all breakpoints, watch variables, or both.
Quit	Terminates the debugger session.
Set variable-expression	Assigns new values to a variable.
Step	Executes statements one at a time.
Watch variable	Suspends DATA step execution when the value of a specified variable has been modified.

Help

The DATA step debugger is very similar to the SCL debugger. A few interesting notes:

- The Help command describes (in detail) the complete syntax and functionality.

- Pmenus are available, with all the options.

- Function keys are defined for some of the common commands (except END!).

- You can define macros of debugger commands. I haven't had time to play with this, but it could be useful.

Here is some information from the Debugger Help.

DATA Step Debugger: Overview

With the DATA step debugger a developer can track down logical errors in a DATA step program as it is actually running. You can :

■ set breakpoints and watched variables whose values display when the program suspends at a breakpoint (WATCH command)

■ examine or even modify the values of variables (EXAMINE command)

■ resume program execution after a program is suspended or after correcting the cause of a program's execution error (GO command)

■ resume program execution from any executable statement (JUMP command)

■ monitor program execution statement by statement (STEP command)

■ display the attributes of a symbol (DESCRIBE command)

■ swap between the DATA step debugger and source windows (SWAP command)

DATA Step Debugger: Commands

Execution GO JUMP QUIT STEP

Display   DESCRIBE EXAMINE LIST

Suspension BREAK DELETE TRACE WATCH

Window   SWAP

Other   CALCULATE ENTER HELP IF SET

How to put variable labels into titles

There are several ways to get a variable label into a title.

1. Use the CALL LABEL function to get the label into a variable and then SYMPUT to put it into a macro variable. The macro variable can then be used in a TITLE statement.

2. Use SQL to get the label from a data dictionary table and into a macro variable.

3. Get it from the SASHELP column view, either in SQL or a DATA step.

Below are examples, each using SASUSER.FITNESS, of each of the 3 methods.

CALL LABEL

```
data _null_ ;
length agelabel $ 40 ;
set sasuser.fitness ;
call label(age,agelabel) ;
call symput("agemacro",agelabel) ;
stop ;
run ;
NOTE: The DATA statement used 0.01 CPU seconds and 1614K.
title "&agemacro" ;
proc print data=sasuser.fitness(obs=1) ;
run ;
NOTE: The PROCEDURE PRINT used 0.01 CPU seconds and 1614K.
```

```
Age in years
OBS   AGE   WEIGHT   RUNTIME   RSTPULSE   RUNPULSE   MAXPULSE   OXYGEN   GROUP
 1    57    73.37    12.63       58         174        176      39.407     2
```

DICTIONARY.COLUMNS

```
proc sql ;
SELECT label into:wmacro
FROM dictionary.columns
WHERE libname='SASUSER'
& memname='FITNESS'
& name='WEIGHT' ;
title "&wmacro" ;
```

```
NOTE: The PROCEDURE SQL used 0.01 CPU seconds and 2720K.
proc print data=sasuser.fitness(obs=1) ;
run ;
NOTE: The PROCEDURE PRINT used 0.01 CPU seconds and 2720K.
```

Weight in kg

OBS	AGE	WEIGHT	RUNTIME	RSTPULSE	RUNPULSE	MAXPULSE	OXYGEN	GROUP
1	57	73.37	12.63	58	174	176	39.407	2

SASHELP.VCOLUMN

```
proc sql ;
SELECT label INTO :gmacro
FROM sashelp.vcolumn
WHERE libname='SASUSER'
& memname='FITNESS'
& name='GROUP' ;
title "&gmacro" ;
NOTE: The PROCEDURE SQL used 0.02 CPU seconds and 2722K.
proc print data=sasuser.fitness(obs=1) ;
run ;
NOTE: The PROCEDURE PRINT used 0.01 CPU seconds and 2722K.
```

Experimental group

OBS	AGE	WEIGHT	RUNTIME	RSTPULSE	RUNPULSE	MAXPULSE	OXYGEN	GROUP
1	57	73.37	12.63	58	174	176	39.407	2

Simple ways to comment out code

Adding the CANCEL option to the RUN statement will prevent a DATA step or PROC step from running. This is useful for disabling a DATA step or PROC step without deleting or commenting the code out. Beware, though, that if the data set does not exist, then the code will still generate an error even though SAS does not attempt to run it.

Log for a PROC example

```
proc contents data=sasuser._all_ ;
run cancel ;

NOTE: The procedure was not executed at the user's request.
NOTE: The PROCEDURE CONTENTS used 0.00 CPU seconds and 1537K.
```

Log for a DATA step example

```
    data ;
       put "This is a test on &sysday" ;
    run ;

This is a test on Friday
NOTE: The data set WORK.DATA1 has 1 observations and 0 vari-
ables.
NOTE: The DATA statement used 0.01 CPU seconds and 1435K.

    data ;
       put "This is a test on &sysday" ;
    run cancel ;

NOTE: Data step not executed at user's request.
NOTE: The DATA statement used 0.00 CPU seconds and 1435K.
```

For more information

See *SAS Language: Reference*, page 479.

Altering processing within a DO loop, based on a condition

Leaving a loop based on a condition

The LEAVE statement ceases processing the current DO loop or SELECT group. Execution continues with the statement following the DO loop or SELECT group. This is very useful should you want to leave a loop (or group) if some condition is met.

There is a trap with nested DO loops in that the LEAVE statement only leaves the current DO loop, not all of the DO loops in which the statement may be nested.

```
data temp ;
  set random ;
  *** Put all the variables starting with x into an array ;
  array scores(*) x: ;
  *** Loop through the variables looking for a score over
90% ;
  do i=1 to dim(scores) ;
    if scores(i)>.9 then
      leave ; *** If we find one then leave the loop ;
  end ;
  put scores(i)= ; *** Write out the score that we ended up
with ;
  run ;

X2=0.9700887157
NOTE: The data set WORK.TEMP has 1 observations and 21 vari-
ables.
NOTE: The DATA statement used 0.02 CPU seconds and 1881K.
```

Going on to the next iteration of a DO loop

The CONTINUE statement stops processing the current iteration of a DO loop and continues with the next iteration. It can be used to terminate processing an iteration based on some condition.

In this example if an element of the CRIMES array is less than 100, then I go on to the next iteration of the loop. Otherwise, I write out information about it.

```
    data over100 ;
       set sasuser.crime(drop=state) ;  * Dont need this variable ;
       array crimes(*) _numeric_ ;       * Put all the crime rates in an
array ;
       do i=1 to dim(crimes) ;          * Loop through each of the crime
variables ;
          if crimes(i)<100 then
             CONTINUE ;                  * If a rate is under 100 then
                                           proceed to next iteration ;
          put 'State: ' staten
              'has ' crimes(i)= ;        * These are >= 100 ;
       end ;
    run ;
```

```
State: Alabama has ASSAULT=278.3
State: Alabama has BURGLARY=1135.5
State: Alabama has LARCENY=1881.9
State: Alabama has AUTO=280.7
State: Alaska has ASSAULT=284
 etc. etc. etc.
```

For more information

For information on the LEAVE statement, see SAS Technical Report P-222, pages 34-35.

For information on the CONTINUE statement, see SAS Technical Report P-222, pages 25-26.

Editing external files in place

You can use PUT statements to make modifications to large external files (flat files, VSAM, etc.) rather than reading data into SAS variables, modifying variables, and writing them out. This also avoids the 200-character limitation on character variables.

There are two ways to accomplish this.

1. Use PUT _INFILE_ to write out the data you read in, and then overwrite the parts you want to change.

2. Use the SHAREBUFFERS option in the INFILE statement to cause the FILE and INFILE statements to use the same buffer. This saves CPU time by eliminating the need to copy the input buffer to the output buffer.

Basic example code:

```
data _null_ ;
  infile 'very-long-recs'
          sharebuffers ;      /* Define input file */
  input ;                     /* Read a record into the input buffer */
  file out ;                  /* Point to where you want to write output */
    put @33  'ABC'            /* write changes */
        @400 '12345'          /* write another change */
        @999 'Wow' ;          /* write the last change */
  run ;
```

Alternate example code:

```
  put _infile_ ',this,that' ;  * Appends 2 fields to the end
of a CSV file ;

  put first ',' second ',' _infile_ ; * Puts 2 fields at the
start of a CSV file ;
```

For more information

See *SAS Programming Tips*, Tip 4.10, page 31.

Also see *SAS Language and Procedures: Usage 2*, page 425-426.

Data of views can't change

If the structure of data sets on which views are based changes, then the view will no longer work. In the following example I create a DATA step view and use it successfully. Then I add a variable to the data set that the view references, and the view no longer works. You must also keep the libref (SASUSER in this example) the same.

```
data v_house / view=v_house ;
   set sasuser.houses ;
run ;

NOTE: DATA STEP view saved on file WORK.V_HOUSE.
NOTE: The original source statements cannot be retrieved from
      a stored DATA STEP view nor will a stored DATA STEP view
      run under a different release of the SAS system or under
      a different operating system.
      Please be sure to save the source statements for this
      DATA STEP view.
NOTE: The DATA statement used 0.44 seconds.


proc print data=v_house(obs=1) ;

NOTE: The view WORK.V_HOUSE.VIEW used 0.39 seconds.

NOTE: The PROCEDURE PRINT used 0.44 seconds.


data sasuser.houses ;
   set sasuser.houses ;
   obs=_n_ ;
run ;

NOTE: The data set SASUSER.HOUSES has 15 observations and 7
variables.
NOTE: The DATA statement used 0.66 seconds.


NOTE: The view WORK.V_HOUSE.VIEW used 0.22 seconds.

proc print data=v_house(obs=1) ;
ERROR: The variable OBS from data set SASUSER.HOUSES is not
defined in the INPUT view WORK.V_HOUSE.
ERROR: Failure loading view WORK.V_HOUSE.VIEW with request 4.
```

BY group processing different for PROC steps and DATA steps

PROC steps versus DATA steps

The default behavior in SAS is that BY groups in the DATA step are defined by unformatted values, whereas BY groups in PROC steps are defined by formatted values.

```
   * Make dataset with a set of 8 different date values ;
   * These only have 3 different formatted values ;
   data x ;
      informat date date7. ;
      format date monname. ; * For example September ;
      input date ;
   cards ;

NOTE: The data set WORK.X has 8 observations and 1 variables.
NOTE: The DATA statement used 0.01 CPU seconds and 2008K.


   ;

   * Sort into ascending order ;
   proc sort data=x ;
      by date ;

   * Summarise by date, which uses the formatted values of
date ;

NOTE: The data set WORK.X has 8 observations and 1 variables.

NOTE: The PROCEDURE SORT used 0.01 CPU seconds and 2008K.

   proc summary data=x nway ;
      by date ;
      output out=y ;
   run ;

NOTE: The data set WORK.Y has 3 observations and 3 variables.
NOTE: The PROCEDURE SUMMARY used 0.01 CPU seconds and 2008K.


   * This prints only 3 values ;
   proc print data=y ;
```

```
  * Read values in, which uses the unformatted value of date ;
  * This can be seen since we write the first value of each BY
group ;
  * and we have 8 BY groups ;

NOTE: The PROCEDURE PRINT used 0.01 CPU seconds and 2008K.

  data z ;
    set x ;
      by date ;
    if first.date then
      put date= ;
  run ;

DATE=September
DATE=September
DATE=September
DATE=October
DATE=October
DATE=November
DATE=November
DATE=November
NOTE: The data set WORK.Z has 8 observations and 1 variables.
NOTE: The DATA statement used 0.01 CPU seconds and 2008K.
```

```
OBS       DATE        _TYPE_      _FREQ_

 1      September        0           3
 2       October         0           2
 3      November         0           3
```

Processing by formatted values in a DATA step

Using the GROUPFORMAT option with the BY statement in a DATA step enables you to
do BY group processing on data which is grouped by formatted values. The FIRST.*variable*
and LAST.*variable* are the first and last observations in the group. This is particularly
handy for grouping numeric data into ranges which can be dealt with separately.

For example, group heights from a class of students (this is the default SAS sample data set
SASUSER.CLASS) into five ranges, then show the shortest in each range.

```
    proc format ;
      value range
      low -55 = 'Under 55'
      55-60   = '55 to 60'
      60-65   = '60 to 65'
      65-70   = '65 to 70'
      other   = 'Over 70' ;
```
NOTE: Format RANGE has been output.

NOTE: The PROCEDURE FORMAT used 0.01 CPU seconds and 1905K.

```
    proc sort data=sasuser.class ;
      by height ;
```

NOTE: Input data set is already sorted, no sorting done.
NOTE: The PROCEDURE SORT used 0.00 CPU seconds and 1905K.

```
    data _null_ ;
      format height range. ;
      set sasuser.class ;
        by groupformat height ;
      if first.height then
      put "Shortest in " height " range measures " height 3.1 ;
    run ;
```

```
Shortest in Under 55   range measures   51
Shortest in 55 to 60   range measures   56
Shortest in 60 to 65   range measures   63
Shortest in 65 to 70   range measures   65
Shortest in Over 70   range measures   72
```
NOTE: The DATA statement used 0.01 CPU seconds and 1905K.

Results of merges differ if a BY statement is used

A MERGE statement with no BY statement works differently than a MERGE statement with a BY statement even if there is only one BY group.

A MERGE statement without a BY statement does a one-to-one merge (*SAS Language: Reference*, page 147). This combines data by observation number and doesn't require data sets to be pre-sorted.

A MERGE statement with a BY statement does a match merge (*SAS Language Reference*, page 151). Data sets must be pre-sorted or indexed, and they are merged based on the values of variables in the BY statement.

n-to-n Match Merging

You can combine data in 6 ways using the DATA step:

1. concatenating

2. interleaving

3. one-to-one reading

4. one-to-one merging

5. match-merging   <=== We will look at this one!

6. updating

When doing a many to many match-merge, SAS reads the first observation from each data set in the same order the data sets appear in the MERGE statement. This means that like-named variables from data sets at the end of the MERGE statement will overwrite values from other like-named variables. See example output below where values of B are taken from data set Y rather than X.

Values from data sets that are being merged are retained during BY group processing. So if you run out of variables from a data set, then MERGE retains the last values of that data set's variables.

```
data x ;
   input a b ;
cards ;
1 2
1 3
1 4
5 99
;

data y ;
   input a b c ;
cards ;
1 6 9
1 7 10
5 8 11
;

data merge ;
   merge x y ;
      by a ;
run ;

proc print ;
```

```
OBS    A    B    C
 1     1    6     9    <=== B is 6, not 2, since it comes from the 2nd dset
 2     1    7    10    <=== B is 7, not 3
 3     1    4    10    <=== C is 10 again, since its value was retained
 4     5    8    11    <=== B is 8, not 99
```

For more information

See *SAS Language: Reference*, pages 151-152.

Values are retained when doing indexed reads

When doing indexed reads, it seems that SAS keeps the values from the last successful read as though they were retained.

To get around this, you must use the _IORC_ automatic variable to determine whether the indexed read was successful or not. _IORC_=0 indicates that the read was successful; _IORC_=1230015 indicates that no match was found.

The example below shows that the first state name ('Nowhere') was *not* found, the second ('Iowa') *was* found and the 3rd (even though *not* found) kept the values from SASUSER.CRIME that were found for 'Iowa'.

```
* Put an index on a dataset for the test ;
proc datasets library=sasuser;
   modify crime ;
   index create staten;

* Make a dataset of values to use for lookup ;
data x ;
   staten='Nowhere' ; output;
   staten='Iowa' ; output;
   staten='Noplace' ; output;
run ;

data y(keep=iorc staten murder rape auto) ;
   set x ; * Read the value to lookup ;
   set sasuser.crime key=staten/unique ; * Use index to lookup
value ;
   iorc=_iorc_ ;
run ;
proc print ;run;
```

OBS	STATEN	MURDER	RAPE	AUTO	IORC
1	Nowhere	.	.	.	1230015
2	Iowa	2.3	10.6	219.9	0
3	Noplace	2.3	10.6	219.9	1230015

Sort before indexed read

When doing an indexed read against a large data set, it is more efficient to sort the transaction data set (the one that is used to determine what to read) into the same order as the data set you are reading from. This means that when a page is read from the "master" data set, there is a better chance that the next thing you read will already be on that page. If it is, then SAS will get the data from memory rather than having to read the page from disk. If the transaction data set is not sorted, then SAS may do unnecessary I/O to the data set.

```
* Sort the transaction dataset by the key ;
Proc sort data=transact ;
  by account ;

Data selectn ;
 * Get account number to look up ;
  set transact ;
 * Look it up ;
  set master key=accno/unique ;
 * If we found it then write the info out ;
  if _iorc_=0 then
     output ;
run ;
```

Views don't use indexes

If you create a view (DATA step or SQL) of an indexed SAS data set, the index of that data set is not used when you use the view.

Log: DATA step view

```
options msglevel=i ; *** Tell me when SAS uses an index ;

proc datasets library=mis ;
  modify item ;
  index create _type_ ;
NOTE: Single index _TYPE_ defined.
run;

NOTE: The PROCEDURE DATASETS used 3.02 seconds.

*** This shows that the index is being used when using the
dataset directly ;
proc print data=mis.item ;
  where _type_=0 ;
INFO: Index _TYPE_ selected for WHERE clause optimization.
run;

NOTE: The PROCEDURE PRINT used 0.22 seconds.

*** Make a DATA step view ;
data v_item / view=v_item ;
  set mis.item ;
  year=substr(servmth,1,2) ;
run ;

NOTE: DATA STEP view saved on file WORK.V_ITEM.
NOTE: The original source statements cannot be retrieved from
a stored DATA STEP view nor
      will a stored DATA STEP view run under a different
release of the SAS system or under
      a different operating system.
      Please be sure to save the source statements for this
DATA STEP view.
NOTE: The DATA statement used 0.55 seconds.

*** Use the DATA step view, and notice that the index is not
used ;
```

```
proc print data=v_item ;
  where _type_=0 ;
run;

NOTE: The view WORK.V_ITEM.VIEW used 1.41 seconds.

NOTE: The PROCEDURE PRINT used 1.59 seconds.
```

Log: SQL view

```
proc sql ;
  create view v_item as
  select *,
          substr(servmth,1,2) as year
  from mis.item ;
NOTE: SQL view WORK.V_ITEM has been defined.
quit ;
NOTE: The PROCEDURE SQL used 0.39 seconds.


proc print data=v_item ;
  where _type_=0 ;
run;

NOTE: The PROCEDURE PRINT used 3.62 seconds.
```

4

Bringing environment variables into macro variables

This tip is very useful for determining system information. In SAS under Windows, UNIX and OS/2, there's a function called SYSGET that gets DOS or SAS environment variables into macro variables. It can also be used as a way to pass from DOS into SAS information which could then be used in SAS programs.

In this example I extract one system environment variable and then two variables that I set in my AUTOEXEC.BAT file.

```
     %let comspec=%sysget(comspec);
     %let temp=%sysget(temp);
     %let name=%sysget(name);
     %put comspec=&comspec ;
comspec=C:\COMMAND.COM
     %put temp=&temp ;
temp=C:\TEMP
     %put name=&name ;
name=Philip Mason
```

For more information

See the *SAS Companion for the Microsoft Windows Environment, Version 6, First Edition*, page 255 (also in OS/2).

Using stored compiled programs

Why? *By compiling a program and storing it away, you save the CPU time used to compile it each time it is run, thereby improving performance.*

From Release 6.06 onwards you can compile DATA steps and save the compiled code to be executed later. The main advantage of this is that you only need to compile the code once but can run it many times, saving resources used in doing the compile each time you run.

4

```
data test / pgm=sasuser.prog1 ;
  set sasuser.class ;
  if age<10 then
    child='YES' ;
run ;

NOTE: DATA STEP program saved on file SASUSER.PROG1.
NOTE: The original source statements cannot be retrieved from
      a stored DATA STEP program nor will a stored DATA STEP
      program run under a different release of the SAS system
      or under a different operating system.
      Please be sure to save the source statements for this
      stored program.
NOTE: The DATA statement used 0.01 CPU seconds and 1600K.

data pgm=sasuser.prog1 ;
run ;

NOTE: DATA STEP program loaded from file SASUSER.PROG1.
NOTE: The data set WORK.TEST has 19 observations and 6 vari-
ables.
NOTE: The DATA statement used 0.01 CPU seconds and 1694K.
```

Treatment of macros

Be aware that when you use compiled programs in SAS together with macro variables, those macro variables are resolved at compile time. This goes for compiled DATA steps and SCL programs. If you want to use the value of a macro variable at execution time, then you should use the SYMGET function.

```
value=SYMGET('macrovar') ; * Specify macro name without a
leading & or % ;
```

For more information

See *SAS Technical Report P-222, Changes and Enhancements to Base SAS Software, Release 6.07*, pages 26-28.

Logic variations using IF & WHERE

Usually the conditions used with an IF and a WHERE will produce the same results but not in all cases.

A SAS trap is not a bug but a feature. Most of them are documented, but often they are counter intuitive and dangerous for even the experienced user. Some are avoidable, some have historical rationales, some are just bizarre. Here is one such trap.

Usually `Where var;` and `If var;` will produce the same result. However, if the value of the variable is a character value of '0' then the WHERE will return TRUE and the IF will return FALSE. The example below demonstrates this.

4

```
data x ;
  zero='0' ;
run ;

NOTE: The data set WORK.X has 1 observations and 1 variables.
NOTE: The DATA statement used 0.01 CPU seconds and 1383K.
data If ;
  set x ;
  if zero ;
run ;

NOTE: Character values have been converted to numeric
values at the places given by: (Line):(Column).
42:6
NOTE: The data set WORK.IF has 0 observations and 1 variables.
NOTE: The DATA statement used 0.01 CPU seconds and 1383K.
data Where ;
  set x ;
    where zero ;
run ;

NOTE: The data set WORK.WHERE has 1 observations and 1 vari-
ables.
NOTE: The DATA statement used 0.01 CPU seconds and 1399K.
```

Note that ZERO is a character variable. The log shows a character-to-numeric conversion with the IF statement. It does not do so with the WHERE statement because "if you use the name of a character variable by itself as a WHERE expression, the SAS system selects observations where the value of the character variable is not blank" (*SAS Language: Reference*, p. 499) and '0' is not blank.

For more information

See *SAS Language: Reference*, page 499.

4

Additional SAS documentation

If you want more information about the tips covered in this section, then try reading the relevant SAS documentation.

These manuals include:

■ *SAS Language and Procedures: Usage 2, Version 6, First Edition*

4

Chapter 5
Macros

5

Automatic macro variables

The SAS System keeps a set of automatic macro variables that can be used by the programmer. They provide information such as the date, current device, completion codes of procedures, and so on. They can be used in DATA steps with the SYMGET function or elsewhere with macro facility commands.

I have found automatic macro variables such as &SYSERR of use in AF applications where I use SUBMIT CONTINUE to submit a SAS procedure and check whether it completed successfully or not.

Log: Very simple example

```
%put Session for &sysjobid started on &sysday &sysdate at
&systime ;
Session for XV02341 started on Thursday 29SEP94 at 06:51
```

Here is a list (from SAS Help) of the automatic macro variables available. Note that different SAS products provide extra automatic macro variables. Also different operating systems have some different automatic macro variables. So your list may vary from the one listed here. A '*' indicates that the variable is read-only.

SYSBUFFR receives text entered in response to a %INPUT statement that the macro processor cannot match with any variable in the statement.

SYSCMD contains the last command from the command line of a macro window that was not recognized by display manager.*

SYSDATE gives the date the job started execution in DATE6. or DATE7. format.*

SYSDAY gives the day of week the job or session started execution.*

SYSDEVIC gives the name of the current graphics device.

SYSDSN gives the name of the most recently created SAS data set.

SYSENV returns FORE if the SAS program was entered from the keyboard. If input does not come from the keyboard, or if the macro executes in noninteractive mode, the value is BACK.*

SYSERR contains the return code set by SAS procedures. Values are:

    0 execution completed successfully

    1 execution canceled by user with a RUN CANCEL statement.

    2 execution canceled by user with an ATTN or BREAK command.

    4 execution completed successfully but with warning messages.

   >4 an error occurred.

SYSFILRC   0 if the last FILENAME statement executed without errors; otherwise, SYS-FILRC is set to the return code of the filename operation.

SYSINDEX   gives the number of macros that have started execution in the current SAS job or session.*

SYSINFO   contains return code information provided by some SAS procedures.

SYSJOBID   gives the name of the currently executing batch job. The value and behavior is system dependent. Please refer to the SAS documentation for your operating system.

SYSLAST   gives the name of the most recently created SAS data set.

SYSLIBRC   contains the return code from the LIBNAME statement.

SYSLCKRC   0 if the last LOCK statement executed without errors; otherwise, SYSLCK-RC is set to the return code of the lock operation.

SYSMENV   gives the currently active macro execution environment.*

Values:

S   macro was part of the SAS program.

D   macro was invoked from display manager or full-screen procedure command line.

SYSMSG   contains a message to be displayed in the message area of a macro window.

SYSPARM   returns the same string as that returned by the DATA step function SYSPARM().

SYSPBUFF   receives all text supplied as macro parameter values in the macro call.

SYSSCP   returns the abbreviation for the operating system being used.*

SYSSCPL   returns the long name for the operating system being used.*

SYSRC   contains the return code from the X statement, X command, or any other operating-system command.

SYSTIME   gives the time the job started execution (hh:mm).*

SYSVER   gives the version of SAS software you are using.

Listing macro variables and their values

In SAS Release 6.11 one can use keywords such as _USER_, _GLOBAL_, _LOCAL_, _AUTOMATIC_, and _ALL_ with %PUT to write macro variables and their values to the log. Only one keyword can be used at a time and there can be no other text in the %PUT statement. _LOCAL_ means local to the current environment. To obtain variables available in the local environment use _USER_ or _ALL_.

```
114   %let mg = i am global ;
115   %macro t ;
116       %local l1 l2 ;
117       %let l2 = i am local ;
118       %q
119   %mend t ;
120   %macro q ;
121       %local l3 ;
122       %let l3 = inner local ;
123       %put ***** local ***** ;
124       %put _local_ ;
125       %put --- user --- ;
126       %put _user_ ;
127       %put ===== all ===== ;
128       %put _all_ ;
129       %mend q ;
130   %t
***** local *****
Q L3 inner local
--- user ---
Q L3 inner local
T L2 i am local
T L1
GLOBAL MG i am global
===== all =====
Q L3 inner local
T L2 i am local
T L1
GLOBAL MG i am global
AUTOMATIC AFDSID 0
AUTOMATIC AFDSNAME
AUTOMATIC AFLIB
AUTOMATIC AFSTR1
AUTOMATIC AFSTR2
AUTOMATIC FSPBDV
AUTOMATIC SYSBUFFR
```

```
AUTOMATIC SYSCMD
AUTOMATIC SYSDATE 12OCT95
AUTOMATIC SYSDAY Thursday
AUTOMATIC SYSDEVIC
AUTOMATIC SYSDSN              _NULL_
AUTOMATIC SYSENV FORE
AUTOMATIC SYSERR 0
AUTOMATIC SYSFILRC 0
AUTOMATIC SYSINDEX 19
AUTOMATIC SYSINFO 0
AUTOMATIC SYSJOBID 0000012383
AUTOMATIC SYSLAST _NULL_
AUTOMATIC SYSLCKRC 0
AUTOMATIC SYSLIBRC 0
AUTOMATIC SYSMENV S
AUTOMATIC SYSMSG
AUTOMATIC SYSPARM
AUTOMATIC SYSPBUFF
AUTOMATIC SYSRC 0
AUTOMATIC SYSSCP WIN
AUTOMATIC SYSSCPL WIN_32S
AUTOMATIC SYSSITE 0009005004
AUTOMATIC SYSTIME 08:08
AUTOMATIC SYSVER 6.11
AUTOMATIC SYSVLONG 6.11.0005P060295
```

Accessing all macro variable values

New to SAS Release 6.11 is a view which shows the contents of the macro symbol table. This is extremely useful in keeping track of macro variables and their definitions. Another new SAS Release 6.11 feature is to use %PUT _ALL_ ; which will list all macro values. The advantage of using the macro table view is that its contents can be used programmatically.

Another source of this information is DICTIONARY.MACROS which is available when using SQL.

Example Log

```
proc print data=sashelp.vmacro ;
run ;

NOTE: The PROCEDURE PRINT used 0.7 seconds.
```

OBS	SCOPE	NAME	OFFSET	VALUE
1	GLOBAL	EXTRAMSG	0	N
2	GLOBAL	SIZFONT	0	3
3	GLOBAL	NUMBLIST	0	5
4	GLOBAL	LOTUSCMD	0	
5	GLOBAL	PRINTLST	0	
6	GLOBAL	TITLELST	0	
7	GLOBAL	DEFFONT	0	arial
8	GLOBAL	EXCELCMD	0	
9	GLOBAL	LIBCATGR	0	work.gseg
10	GLOBAL	WCLSCTRY	0	
11	GLOBAL	LOGACCES	0	
12	GLOBAL	EISPATH	0	c:\sas
13	GLOBAL	LANGLIST	0	eisita.utility.english.slist
14	GLOBAL	EISITA	0	c:\Sas\motore
15	GLOBAL	GOPTSTR	0	
16	GLOBAL	DEBUG	0	1
17	GLOBAL	MOTRELST	0	0
18	AUTOMATIC	AFDSID	0	0
19	AUTOMATIC	AFDSNAME	0	
20	AUTOMATIC	AFLIB	0	
21	AUTOMATIC	AFSTR1	0	

22	AUTOMATIC	AFSTR2	0	
23	AUTOMATIC	FSPBDV	0	
24	AUTOMATIC	SYSBUFFR	0	
25	AUTOMATIC	SYSCMD	0	
26	AUTOMATIC	SYSDATE	0	24OCT95
27	AUTOMATIC	SYSDAY	0	Tuesday
28	AUTOMATIC	SYSDEVIC	0	WIN
29	AUTOMATIC	SYSDSN	0	_NULL_
30	AUTOMATIC	SYSENV	0	FORE
31	AUTOMATIC	SYSERR	0	0
32	AUTOMATIC	SYSFILRC	0	0
33	AUTOMATIC	SYSINDEX	0	0
34	AUTOMATIC	SYSINFO	0	0
35	AUTOMATIC	SYSJOBID	0	0000006399
36	AUTOMATIC	SYSLAST	0	_NULL_
37	AUTOMATIC	SYSLCKRC	0	0
38	AUTOMATIC	SYSLIBRC	0	0
39	AUTOMATIC	SYSMENV	0	
40	AUTOMATIC	SYSMSG	0	
41	AUTOMATIC	SYSPARM	0	
42	AUTOMATIC	SYSPBUFF	0	
43	AUTOMATIC	SYSRC	0	0
44	AUTOMATIC	SYSSCP	0	WIN
45	AUTOMATIC	SYSSCPL	0	WIN_32S
46	AUTOMATIC	SYSSITE	0	0002582050
47	AUTOMATIC	SYSTIME	0	07:09
48	AUTOMATIC	SYSVER	0	6.11
49	AUTOMATIC	SYSVLONG	0	6.11.0005P060295

Arithmetic calculations in macros

The macro language compares numbers with dot characters (decimal points) as character strings. The EVAL macro function returns 1 (for true) when calculating 2<10, but returns 0 (false) when we add a dot character (decimal point) to the end of the numbers.

```
%put =======> %eval(2<10) ;
=======> 1

%put =======> %eval(2.<10.) ;
=======> 0
```

%EVAL always evaluates digit-strings as integers, even if they are quoted. Hence, long digit-strings will cause overflow. The following example raises 9 to the power 99, which causes an overflow error.

```
%put =======> %eval(9**99) ;
ERROR: Overflow has occurred; evaluation is terminated.
```

Match quotes in macro comments

Quotes must be matched if they are used in macro comments - this doesn't apply to other comments. If they are not matched then SAS searches for the next quote before it deals with any other code. This can lead to unexpected and confusing errors.

Note also that /* */ comments are slightly more efficient than macro comments, so when you have a choice, use /* */ comments. Another reason to use /* */ comments rather than macro comments is because of the inconsistent way in which macro comments treat quote marks.

SAS gives you a clue that you may have unbalanced quotes when it finds more than 200 characters between your quotes; you will get the following warning:

```
WARNING: The current word or quoted string has become more
         than 200 characters long.  You may have unbalanced
         quotation marks.
```

So, make sure your quotes are matched. The following example demonstrates unmatched quotes.

```
%* This is Phil's unmatched quote which will cause problems ;

data x ;
  put "This single quote ' will not match with the previous
one'" ;
 * since it was in quotes ;
  put 'But the first one used here will' ;
 * Note there is one single quote left unmatched ;
run ;

 * These quotes "' are O.K., since this kind of comment does-
n't mind ;
/* These quotes '" are also O.K., since these comments don't
mind either */
```

Quotes in non-macro comments outside of macros do not need to be matched.

```
 * This comment has 1 quote ' and is O.K. ;
proc print data=sasuser.crime(obs=1) ;
run ;
```

Quotes in macros or macro statements, including macro comments, need to be matched unless you use something like %STR(%').

```
%* This is not OK ' ;
proc print data=sasuser.crime(obs=1) ;
run ;
WARNING: The current word or quoted string has become more
than 200
characters long.  You may have unbalanced quotation marks.
%* because the proc print ends up between quotes ' and never
runs ;
```

5

Forcing SAS to store macro symbol tables on disk

Macro symbol tables are usually stored in memory; however, specifying OPTIONS MSYMTABMAX=0 will cause them to be stored to disk. Global macro variables will be stored in WORK.SASST0. Local macro variables will be stored in a series of catalogs starting with WORK.SASST1. This enables a program to be written to obtain the macro variable names for each environment and then to use the SYMGET function to obtain their values.

There are some macro variable values which are not available in this way, for instance, variables in a %DO expression such as `%do i=1 %to 10 ;` In this case the macro variable &I would not be available in the disk file, since it is only kept in memory.

Example Code

```
* Store macro symbol table to work library ;
options msymtabmax=0 ;

*** Define some macro variables ;
%let a=1 ;
%let b=2 ;

%macro fred ;
   %let c=3 ;
%mend fred ;

%fred

*** Now look in your Work library and you can see the SASSTn
catalogs ;
***     each one has a member for each macro variable ;
```

How to produce files for import into other applications

Here is a macro that can be used to create a tab-separated file for import into Microsoft EXCEL (Lotus 123, Microsoft Access, etc.) from a SAS data set. The macro uses TABS to separate fields, rather than commas, to avoid any problem with data that may contain commas.

Be aware that the hex value for a tab character varies depending on the platform being used. On ASCII systems it is '09'X; however, on EBCDIC systems (such as IBM mainframes) it is '05'X.

You can invoke the macro with data set options if you wish to use only certain variables or to apply a WHERE clause to select certain data.

Here are the data set options.

Positional Parameters

Note that the positional parameters are required and must come before any optional keywords when calling the macro.

DSET   SAS data set name

CSV   filename (DDname in MVS) that exported data is written to

Optional Keyword parameters (specify with an '=')

LIMIT   Only write out this many observations, useful when testing.

TITLE   Write this line at the top of the output file.

EXTRA   Call the macro named here; useful for doing special processing such as applying formats.

Example Code

```
%MAKETSV(saslib.sample(keep=name address where=(name>'L')),csv)

%MAKETSV(saslib.sample,dd1,title=Report number 1,limit=20)
```

Macro Source Code

```
%macro maketsv(dset,csv,limit=,title=,extra=) ;

options nodate nocenter ;

* put the structure of the dataset into a sas data set;
proc contents data=&dset
              out=zxcvbnm1
              noprint ;
run ;

* Sort the data set containing the structure by variable number ;
proc sort data=zxcvbnm1
          out=zxcvbnm2(keep=name) ;
  by varnum ;
run ;

proc transpose data=zxcvbnm2
               out=zxcvbnm3(drop=_name_ _label_) ;
  var name ;
run ;

data _null_ ;
  set zxcvbnm3 ;
  file &csv ;

* Note the two semi-colons, one for the PUT statement
                         and one for the %IF statement ;
  %if &title ne %then
    put "&title" ; ;

  put (_all_) ( +(-1) '05'x ) ;
run ;

data _null_ ;
  set &dset ;
  file &csv mod ;

%if &limit>0 %then
  %do ;
    if _n_>&limit then
    stop ;
  %end ;

%if &extra> %then
  %&extra ;

* This hex constant is the TAB character for EBCDIC,
* the TAB character for ASCII is '09'X ;
  put (_all_) ( +(-1) '05'x ) ;
run ;

%mend maketsv ;
```

Useful merge macro

Here is a potentially useful macro for general purpose merging. You can use it to modify the default behaviour of the MERGE statement when used without a BY statement.

This macro is particularly useful for data representing a series of measurments over time. If measurements are missing then the previous non-missing value will be used in the merge.

Macro code

```
%****** mergeby ******;
%* mergeby acts like a MERGE statement with a BY statement
even if there are no BY variables;

%macro mergeby(data1, data2, byvars);
  %if %bquote(&byvars) NE %then
    %do;
      merge %unquote(&data1) %unquote(&data2);
        by %unquote(&byvars);
    %end;
  %else
    %do;
      if _end1 & _end2 then
        stop;
      if ^_end1 then
        set %unquote(&data1) end=_end1;
      if ^_end2 then
        set %unquote(&data2) end=_end2;
    %end;
%mend mergeby;
```

Example Code

```
* Create some sample data - firstly dataset x ;
data x;
  do x=1 to 5;
    output;
  end;
run;

* Create some sample data - secondly dataset y ;
data y;
  do y=1 to 3;
    output;
  end;
run;
```

```
*** Now we merge the two datasets with a standard merge state-
ment ;
*** - notice that there is no BY statement ;
data xy;
   merge x y;

proc print;
run;

*** Now we merge the two datasets with the MERGEBY macro ;
data xy;
   %mergeby(x,y);

proc print;
run;
```

Example Output

```
OBS     X     Y

 1      1     1
 2      2     2
 3      3     3
 4      4     .
 5      5     .


OBS     X     Y

 1      1     1
 2      2     2
 3      3     3
 4      4     3
 5      5     3
4
```

Another way to accomplish this is by using the following non-macro code. This has the dis-
advantage that it must be recoded each time.

Example Code

```
data xy(drop=last_y) ;
   retain last_y ;
   merge x y ;
   if y NE . then
      last_y=y ;
   else
      y=last_y ;
run ;
```

Additional SAS documentation

If you want more information about the tips covered in this section then try reading the relevant SAS documentation.

These manuals include:

- *SAS Macro Facility Tips and Techniques, Version 6, First Edition*
- *SAS Guide to Macro Processing, Version 6, Second Edition*

Chapter 6
Assorted Procedure Tips

6

Outputting multiple PROCs to one page

Sometimes the output from a procedure will only use a few lines, which can result in a lot of wasted paper. This tip tells you how to avoid that.

You can stop SAS from going to a new page each time a procedure finishes by changing the character that it uses for jumping to a new page (on MVS this is a 1). Setting the FORMDLIM option to a blank replaces the new-page character with a blank.

```
* Setting it to a space causes SAS to fill each page before
going to the next one ;
Options formdlim=' ' ;

* Setting it to a null string resets the value of formdlim to
the default,
   so that each new Proc will start on a new page ;
Options formdlim='' ;
```

6

Printing graphs in landscape or portrait

If your printer is set to print in portrait mode by default, then graphs will also come out that way. This tip tells you how to make the graphs come out in landscape mode so that they fit the page better.

If your graphs come out portrait rather than landscape when printing them from Windows, then try:

```
GOPTIONS ROTATE ;
```

This will rotate the graph, whereas page orientation (landscape/portrait) only applies to text. Use NOROTATE to get back to unrotated graphics.

In SAS Release 6.10 and prior releases, this technique can be used to make graphs printed from graphics objects in FRAME entries rotate when they are printed. However from SAS Release 6.11 on, this technique does not work for graphics objects.

Putting BY variables into titles

Since SAS Release 6.07 (SAS Technical Report P-222, pages 159-162) you have been able to insert the labels and/or values of BY variables into titles. For the following example, suppose you have a data set sorted by the variable ST, with label "STATE" and formatted values "Victoria," "Tasmania," and so on. Note also that specifying the option NOBYLINE will force a page eject after each BY group.

One BY variable

```
OPTIONS NOBYLINE;

PROC PRINT;
TITLE "List for #BYVAR1 - #BYVAL1";
BY ST;
VAR Var1-Var10;
```

For each BY group, you'll get titles such as the following:

```
List for STATE - Tasmania
List for STATE - Victoria
```

The NOBYLINE option suppresses the printing of the BY lines as part of the output, so you don't also see

```
BY STATE=Tasmania
BY STATE=Victoria
```

You can turn BY lines back on with OPTIONS BYLINE;.

Two BY variables

Assume you have the variables DIV and DEPT, where DEPT is nested within DIV. DIV has one formatted value "Academic Affairs," with DEPTs "Art" and "History," and another formatted value "Administration," with DEPTs "Admissions" and "Registrar."

```
BY DIV DEPT;
TITLE "Budget - #BYVAL1/#BYVAL2";
```

Partial Output

```
Budget - Academic Affairs/Art
Budget - Academic Affairs/History
Budget - Administration/Admissions
Budget - Administration/Registrar
```

Multiple graphs on a page

To put multiple graphs on a page and add titles to graphs in a catalog, Warren Sarle of SAS Institute has kindly provided some macros that are helpful for such things. You can look for these in the SAS online samples available by using one of three facilities: Anonymous FTP, SASDOC-L, or the World Wide Web. See the inside back cover for details.

```
/****************************************************************

      name: grid
     title: Replay graphs in a regular grid
   product: graph
    system: all
     procs: greplay gslide
   support: saswss                              update:   10jul95
```

DISCLAIMER:

        THIS INFORMATION IS PROVIDED BY SAS INSTITUTE INC. AS A SERVICE TO
ITS USERS.   IT IS PROVIDED "AS IS".   THERE ARE NO WARRANTIES, EXPRESSED OR
IMPLIED, AS TO MERCHANTABILITY OR FITNESS FOR A PARTICULAR PURPOSE REGARD-
ING THE ACCURACY OF THE MATERIALS OR CODE CONTAINED HEREIN.

The %GRID macro lets you easily replay graphs in a regular grid with one
or more rows and one or more columns. The %GRID macro also supports titles
and footnotes for the entire replayed graph. For example, if you have run
GPLOT four times and want to replay these graphs in a 2-by-2 grid with the
title 'Four Marvellous Graphs', you could submit the following statements:

```
    title 'Four Marvellous Graphs';
    %grid( gplot*4, rows=2, cols=2);
```

The %GRID macro allows 10% of the vertical size of the graph for titles by
default. You can adjust this percentage via the TOP= argument in %GRID.
Determining the best value for TOP= requires trial and error in most
cases. To allow space for footnotes, use the BOTTOM= argument.

The graphs to replay must be stored in a graphics catalog with library and
member names specified by the macro variables glibrary and &gout. By
default, SAS/GRAPH stores graphs in WORK.GSEG, which is the catalog that
the %GRID macro uses by default. If your graphs are in another catalog,
you must specify &glibrary and/or &gout using %LET statements as
shown below.

Each graph that is stored in a catalog has a name. Each procedure assigns
default names such as GPLOT, GPLOT1, GPLOT2, etc. Most SAS/GRAPH procedures let you specify the name via a NAME= option which takes a quoted
string that must be a valid SAS name. However, if a graph by that name
already exists in the catalog, SAS/GRAPH appends a number to the name; it
does not replace the previous graph by the same name unless you specify

GOPTIONS GOUTMODE=REPLACE, but this option causes _all_ entries in the
catalog to be deleted every time you save a new graph, so it is not very
useful. If you want to replace a single graph in a catalog, sometimes you
can use the %GDELETE macro to delete the old one and later recreate a
graph with the same name, but this does not work reliably due to a bug in
SAS/GRAPH. By default, %GDELETE deletes _everything_ in the catalog; this
does seem to work reliably.

When you use BY processing, SAS/GRAPH appends numbers to the graph name to
designate graphs for each BY group. For example, if you run GPLOT with
three BY groups and NAME='HENRY', the graphs are named HENRY, HENRY1, and
HENRY2. The %GRID macro lets you abbreviate this list of names as HENRY*3,
where the repetition factor following the asterisk is the total number of
graphs, not the number of the last graph.

        ***/

```
%let glibrary=WORK;
%let gout=GSEG;

%macro grid(   /* replay graphs in a rectangular grid */
    list,      /* list of names of graphs, separated by blanks;
                  a name may be followed by an asterisk and a
                  repetition factor with no intervening blanks;
                  for example, ABC*3 is expanded to: ABC ABC1 ABC2 */
    rows=1,    /* number of rows in the grid */
    cols=1,    /* number of columns in the grid */
    top=10,    /* percentage at top to reserve for titles */
    bottom=0); /* percentage at bottom to reserve for footnotes */

    %gtitle;
    %greplay;
    %tdef(rows=&rows,cols=&cols,top=&top,bottom=&bottom)
    %trep(&list,rows=&rows,cols=&cols)
    run; quit;
%mend grid;


%macro gdelete(list); /* delete list of graphs from the catalog;
                         default is _ALL_ */

    %if %bquote(&list)= %then %let list=_ALL_;
    proc greplay igout=&glibrary..&gout nofs;
        delete &list;
    run; quit;
%mend gdelete;


%macro gtitle; /* create graph with titles and footnotes only */
```

```
        %global titlecnt;
        %if %bquote(&titlecnt)= %then %let titlecnt=1;
                           %else %let titlecnt=%eval(&titlecnt+1);
        goptions nodisplay;
        proc gslide gout=&glibrary..&gout name="title&titlecnt";
        run;
        goptions display;
    %mend gtitle;


    %macro greplay(  /* invoke PROC GREPLAY */
        tc);          /* template catalog; default is JUNK */

        %if %bquote(&tc)= %then %let tc=junk;
        proc greplay nofs tc=&tc;
            igout &glibrary..&gout;
    %mend greplay;


    %macro tdef(   /* define a template for a rectangular grid */
        rows=1,      /* number of rows in the grid */
        cols=1,      /* number of columns in the grid */
        top=10,      /* percentage at top to reserve for titles */
        bottom=0); /* percentage at bottom to reserve for footnotes */
        %global tdefname; /* returned: name of template */

        %local height width n row col lower upper left right;
        %let height=%eval((100-&top-&bottom)/&rows);
        %let width =%eval(100/&cols);
        %let tdefname=t&rows._&cols;
        tdef &tdefname
            0/ulx=0 uly=100 llx=0 lly=0 urx=100 ury=100 lrx=100 lry=0
        %let n=1;
        %do row=1 %to &rows;
            %let lower=%eval(100-&top-&row*&height);
            %let upper=%eval(&lower+&height);
            %do col=1 %to &cols;
                %let right=%eval(&col*&width);
                %let left =%eval(&right-&width);
                &n/ulx=&left uly=&upper llx=&left lly=&lower
                    urx=&right ury=&upper lrx=&right lry=&lower
                %let n=%eval(&n+1);
            %end;
        %end;
        ;
        template &tdefname;
    %mend tdef;


    %macro trep( /* replay graphs using template defined by %TDEF */
        list,     /* list of names of graphs, separated by blanks;
                     a name may be followed by an asterisk and a
                     repetition factor with no intervening blanks;
                     for example, ABC*3 is expanded to: ABC ABC1 ABC2 */
        rows=,    /* (optional) number of rows in template */
```

```
    cols=);    /* (optional) number of columns in template */
                  /* rows= and cols= default to values set with %TDEF */

  %global titlecnt;
  %local i l n row col name root suffix nrep;
  %if %bquote(&rows)= %then %let rows=%scan(&tdefname,1,t_);
  %if %bquote(&cols)= %then %let cols=%scan(&tdefname,2,t_);
  treplay 0:title&titlecnt
  %let nrep=0;
  %let l=0;
  %let n=0;
  %do row=1 %to &rows;
      %do col=1 %to &cols;
          %let n=%eval(&n+1);
          %if &nrep %then %do;
              %let suffix=%eval(&suffix+1);
              %if &suffix>=&nrep %then %do;
                  %let nrep=0;
                  %goto tryagain;
              %end;
              %let name=&root&suffix;
              %goto doit;
          %end;
%tryagain:
          %let l=%eval(&l+1);
          %let name=%qscan(&list,&l,%str( ));
          %if &name= %then %goto break;
          %let i=%index(&name,*);
          %if &i %then %do;
              %let nrep=%substr(&name,&i+1);
              %if &nrep<=0 %then %goto tryagain;
              %let root=%substr(&name,1,&i-1);
              %let name=&root;
              %let suffix=0;
          %end;
%doit:
          &n:&name
      %end;
  %end;
%break:
  ;
%mend trep;

 /******* Examples for the %GRID macro *******/

%inc greplay;

data trig;
    do n=1 to 100;
        x1=sin(n/16);
        x2=sin(n/8);
        y1=cos(n/16);
        y2=cos(n/8);
```

```
        output;
    end;
run;

goptions nodisplay;
proc gplot data=trig;
    title 'Y1 by X1';
    plot y1*x1;
run;
    title 'Y1 by X2';
    plot y1*x2;
run;
    title 'Y2 by X1';
    plot y2*x1;
run;
    title 'Y2 by X2';
    plot y2*x2;
run;

title 'Four Marvellous Graphs';
%grid( gplot*4, rows=2, cols=2);


title 'Adding a Title to a Single Graph';
footnote 'And a Footnote';
%grid( gplot, top=12, bottom=5);
```

Inconsistent treatment of misspelled PROC names

Sometimes SAS forgives you, sometimes it doesn't. I'm not sure how it decides though.

In the following example SETINIT is derived from SETINITXXXXXXXXXX.

```
      proc setinitxxxxxxxxxx ;run;
      ─────────
          1
Original site validation data
Site name:    'SAS INSTITUTE AUSTRALIA PTY LTD'.
Site number:  2582050.
Expiration:   15JAN96.
Grace Period: 0 days (ending 15JAN96).
Warning Period: 30 days (ending 14FEB96).
System birthday:   23NOV92.
Operating System:  WIN      .
Product expiration dates:
—BASE Product               15JAN96 (CPU A)
—SAS/GRAPH                  15JAN96 (CPU A)
—SAS/ETS                    15JAN96 (CPU A)
—SAS/FSP                    15JAN96 (CPU A)
—SAS/AF                     15JAN96 (CPU A)
—SAS/CALC                   15JAN96 (CPU A)
—SAS/ASSIST                 15JAN96 (CPU A)
—SAS/CONNECT                15JAN96 (CPU A)
—SAS/INSIGHT                15JAN96 (CPU A)
—SAS/EIS                    15JAN96 (CPU A)
—SAS/ACC-ODBC               15JAN96 (CPU A)

WARNING 1-322: Assuming the symbol SETINIT was misspelled as
               SETINITXXXXXXXXXX.

NOTE: The PROCEDURE SETINITXXXXXXXX used 1.27 seconds.
```

In this example OPTIONS is derived from OPTIONSOPTIONSOPTIONS.

```
10    proc optionsoptionsoptions ;run;
      ─────────────
            1

WARNING 1-322: Assuming the symbol OPTIONS was misspelled as
               OPTIONSOPTIONSOPTIONS.

   SAS (r) Proprietary Software Release 6.11   TS005

<lines removed>

NOTE: The PROCEDURE OPTIONSOPTIONSOP used 8.01 seconds.
```

In the next example SAS can't work out that we really meant to type PROC PRINT.

```
20    pro cprint data=sasuser.crime ;
      ───
       14
ERROR: Procedure CPRINT not found.
21    run ;

WARNING 14-169: Assuming the symbol PROC was misspelled as
PRO.

NOTE: The SAS System stopped processing this step because of
errors.
NOTE: The PROCEDURE CPRINT used 0.28 seconds.
```

Additional SAS documentation

If you want more information about the tips covered in this section, then try reading the relevant SAS documentation.

These manuals include:

- *SAS Language and Procedures: Usage 2, Version 6, First Edition*

6

Chapter 7
Utility Procedure Tips

7

More information on space used by catalog members

In PROC CATALOG you can use the undocumented STAT option in the CONTENTS statement to give you space used by catalog members.

Example Code

```
options ls=132 ; * Set linesize wide or output looks a bit
weird ;
PROC CATALOG C=sashelp.eis ;
  CONTENTS STAT ;
run ;
```

Left side of output

#	Name	Type	Date	Description
1	ADDOBJ	CBT	04/06/94	EIS: Add a new object type
2	ADDOBJ2	CBT	04/06/94	EIS: Browse Attribute Definition
3	APPLDS	CBT	04/06/94	EIS: CBT for setup applications
4	APPLICAT	CBT	04/06/94	ASSIST: CBT for EIS builder
5	APPLSEL	CBT	04/06/94	HELP: List of applications in data set

Right side of Output

Page Size	Block Size	Num of Blocks	Last Block Bytes	Last Block Size	Pages
6144	6144	3	125	256	3
6144	6144	2	2588	6144	2
6144	6144	5	4041	6144	5
6144	6144	1	4833	6144	1
6144	1024	4	178	256	1

7 ways to tune sorts in SAS

The SORT procedure is one of the most resource intensive procedures within SAS due to the nature of what it does. It is, therefore, quite important to make it run as efficiently as possible, since large savings can be made here.

There are various ways to make your sort go better. Here are just a few.

1. If you're doing a SORT and you don't require the data within BY groups to be kept in the same order as it was before the sort, then use the NOEQUALS option. This will save you CPU and elapsed time, particularly on very large data sets. This option causes SAS not to worry about keeping observations with the same BY variable values in the same order.

   ```
   PROC SORT data=fred NOEQUALS ;
     BY this that ;
   ```

2. Specify more sort data sets. Often the default is three but you can have up to six data sets. Specify `options sortwkno=6 ;`

3. Use cartridges, tapes or some other form of mass-storage for your sort work data sets. Specify `options sortdev=device-unit-name`. You will rarely run out of space doing this. MVS users note that SMS has a dataclass that stores a tape data set on disk while being used, but quickly archives it off to tape.

4. You can use `options sortsize=max` to tell PROC SORT it can use all available main storage.

5. On MVS you can use Hiperspace or VIO if you have sufficient virtual storage for the amount of data you are sorting. This will speed it up immensely. On Windows or OS/2 this would be similar to using a RAM disk for your sort work data sets.

6. From Release 6.07 onwards, SAS data sets have a sort indicator which indicates that a data set is already sorted. Then if the data is sorted with PROC SORT in the same order, SAS does not do the sort. Look up the SORTEDBY= data set option. This allows you to tell the SAS System the sort order of data that is read from external sources, without running it through PROC SORT.

7. If your data is grouped but not sorted ascending or descending, then often you don't need to sort. Just use the NOTSORTED option in the BY statement.

Eliminating duplicates from a sort

You might expect a SORT with NODUPLICATES specified to remove all duplicate records from the data being sorted. This is not always the case though.

As it says in the *SAS Procedures Guide*, PROC SORT with the NODUPKEY option will remove observations with duplicate BY values from the data set. PROC SORT with the NODUPLICATES option will remove adjacent duplicate observations.

The tip is that SAS looks for adjacent duplicate observations as it writes the output data set from the sort. Many people have the understanding that SAS looks for duplicate adjacent observations in the INPUT data set - this is wrong.

As you can see from the example that follows, we can drop different numbers of duplicates from the same data set just by sorting it into a different order. This is because the output data set has a different sequence when we sort with a BY variable.

```
1          DATA X ;
2          A='X';B='P';C='Q';D='W';OUTPUT;
3          A='X';B='P';C='Q';D='W';OUTPUT;
4          A='X';B='P';C='Q';D='W';OUTPUT;
5          A='X';B='P';C='Q';D='W';OUTPUT;
6          A='X';B='P';C='Q';D='W';OUTPUT;
7          A='X';B='@';C='Q';D='W';OUTPUT;
8          A='X';B='P';C='Q';D='W';OUTPUT;
9          A='X';B='P';C='*';D='W';OUTPUT;
10         A='X';B='P';C='F';D='W';OUTPUT;
11         A='X';B='P';C='F';D='W';OUTPUT;
12         A='X';B='P';C='Q';D='W';OUTPUT;
13         RUN ;

NOTE: The data set WORK.X has 11 observations and 4 vari-
ables.
NOTE: The DATA statement used 0.03 CPU seconds and 1341K.

14
15         PROC SORT DATA=X OUT=A NODUPLICATES ;
16            BY A ;
17
```

7

```
NOTE: 5 duplicate observations were deleted.
NOTE: The data set WORK.A has 6 observations and 4 variables.
NOTE: The PROCEDURE SORT used 0.01 CPU seconds and 1616K.

18          PROC SORT DATA=X OUT=B NODUPLICATES ;
19            BY A B ;
20

NOTE: 6 duplicate observations were deleted.
NOTE: The data set WORK.B has 5 observations and 4 variables.
NOTE: The PROCEDURE SORT used 0.01 CPU seconds and 1620K.

21          PROC SORT DATA=X OUT=C NODUPLICATES ;
22            BY A B C ;
23

NOTE: 7 duplicate observations were deleted.
NOTE: The data set WORK.C has 4 observations and 4 variables.
NOTE: The PROCEDURE SORT used 0.01 CPU seconds and 1620K.

24          PROC SORT DATA=X OUT=D NODUPLICATES ;
25            BY A B C D ;
26

NOTE: 7 duplicate observations were deleted.
NOTE: The data set WORK.D has 4 observations and 4 variables.
NOTE: The PROCEDURE SORT used 0.01 CPU seconds and 1620K.

27          PROC SORT DATA=X OUT=A NODUPKEY ;
28            BY A ;
29

NOTE: 10 observations with duplicate key values were deleted.
NOTE: The data set WORK.A has 1 observations and 4 variables.
NOTE: The PROCEDURE SORT used 0.01 CPU seconds and 1620K.

30          PROC SORT DATA=X OUT=B NODUPKEY ;
31            BY A B ;
32

NOTE: 9 observations with duplicate key values were deleted.
NOTE: The data set WORK.B has 2 observations and 4 variables.
NOTE: The PROCEDURE SORT used 0.01 CPU seconds and 1620K.

33          PROC SORT DATA=X OUT=C NODUPKEY ;
34            BY A B C ;
35
```

```
NOTE: 7 observations with duplicate key values were deleted.
NOTE: The data set WORK.C has 4 observations and 4 variables.
NOTE: The PROCEDURE SORT used 0.01 CPU seconds and 1620K.

36              PROC SORT DATA=X OUT=D NODUPKEY ;
37                BY A B C D ;

NOTE: 7 observations with duplicate key values were deleted.
NOTE: The data set WORK.D has 4 observations and 4 variables.
NOTE: The PROCEDURE SORT used 0.01 CPU seconds and 1620K.
```

7

Copying a file and its indexes

PROC COPY or the COPY statement of PROC DATASETS will maintain indexes when SAS data sets are copied from disk to disk but not when data sets are copied from disk to tape.

Applies to MVS, VMS & CMS.

For more information

See SAS Usage Note V6-SYS.SYS-3637.

7

Additional SAS documentation

If you want more information about the tips covered in this section, then try reading the relevant SAS documentation.

These manuals include:

■ *SAS Language and Procedures: Usage 2, Version 6, First Edition*

7

Chapter 8
Procedure Tips for Displaying Data

8

Creating tab-separated output using PROC TABULATE

You may want to get data from SAS to a database or spreadsheet as quickly as possible. This is a "quick and dirty" method for doing that.

PROC TABULATE can be used to quickly put data out in a form suitable for import into EXCEL.

When you specify the FORMCHAR keyword equal to a comma followed by 10 blanks, the table is put out with a comma separating each column. Alternatively, you can specify a hex value for FORMCHAR if you want to use tabs rather than commas for separating text. In EBCDIC that hex value then would be '0540404040404040404040'X. In ASCII the hex value would be '0920202020202020202020'X.

Additionally, specify the following:

NOSEPS	to get rid of horizontal divider lines
NODATE option	to get rid of date from output
NONUMBER option	to get rid of page numbers
LINESIZE=254	to allow for a wide page
PAGESIZE=32767	to avoid carriage control for new pages; specifying this makes each page this long; 32767 is the maximum value allowed.

You can use PROC PRINTTO FILE=*ddname*; to send the procedure output to a file; or you can specify an external print file using the PRINT option at startup.

```
options nodate
        nonumber
        ls=254
        ps=32767 ;
proc tabulate data=sample
              formchar=',
              noseps ;
   class this that ;
   var num ;
   table sum*num, this all, that all ;
run ;
```

Note that this technique doesn't work as well with multi-dimensional tables.

Producing multi-panel reports with PROC REPORT

PROC REPORT has the ability to show multiple logical pages on one physical page. This feature can be used to save paper.

The PANELS=x option (default is 1) breaks the page into x horizontal panels. The PSPACE=y option (default is 4) puts y spaces between panels. Setting the value of PAN-ELS to a large number will cause SAS to fit as many panels on the page as it can. For example, PANELS=99 might result in two or three panels.

```
proc report data=sasuser.crime
            panels=2 /* 2 horizontal panels */
            nowd ;      * nowd for running in batch ;
   col (staten rape) ; * Define columns we want ;
run ;

NOTE: Procedure REPORT has created 1 page(s) of output so far.
```

```
                         The SAS System                    29
                                  12:37 Monday, June 26, 1995

        State name         RAPE   State name          RAPE
        Alabama            25.2   Kentucky            19.1
        Alaska             51.6   Louisiana           30.9
        Arizona            34.2   Maine               13.5
        Arkansas           27.6   Maryland            34.8
        California         49.4   Massachusetts       20.8
        Colorado           42     Michigan            38.9
        Connecticut        16.8   Minnesota           19.5
        Delaware           24.9   Mississippi         19.6
        Florida            39.6   Missouri            28.3
        Georgia            31.1   Montana             16.7
        Hawaii             25.5   Nebraska            18.1
        Idaho              19.4   Nevada              49.1
        Illinois           21.8   New Hampshire       10.7
        Indiana            26.5   New Jersey          21
        Iowa               10.6   New Mexico          39.1
        Kansas             22     New York            29.4
```

Indenting output using PROC TABULATE

From SAS Release 6.10 onwards, PROC TABULATE supports the INDENT option. This enables nested row-titles to be indented, rather than displayed in separate columns, in order to save space and improve appearance.

Example code

```
options nocenter ;

data sample ;
  length x y $ 1 ;
  input x y z ;

cards ;
a b 1
b c 2
a c 3
a b 4
b c 5
a c 6
;

proc tabulate data=sample ;
  class x y ;
  var z ;
  table x*y, z*(min mean max) / INDENT=3 ;
run ;
```

		z		
		MIN	MEAN	MAX
a				
	b	1.00	2.50	4.00
	c	3.00	4.50	6.00
b				
	c	2.00	3.50	5.00

For more information

See *SAS Software: Changes & Enhancements, Release 6.10*, page 34.

8

Wrapping lines with PROC REPORT

PROC REPORT can group variables together by observation. If the variables don't fit on one line, then they will continue on the next line. PROC REPORT can also prefix the value of each variable with its variable name, to improve clarity.

PROC REPORT statement options

WRAP   keeps values for an observation together, rather than continuing them on the next page.

NAMED puts each variable label/name and an equal sign before each value.

Program using WRAP

```
proc report data=sasuser.crime
            WRAP        /* wrap lines */
            nowd ;      * nowd for running in batch ;
   run ;
```

State name	FIPS code	MURDER	RAPE	ROBBERY	ASSAULT
BURGLARY	LARCENY	AUTO			
Alabama		1	14.2	25.2	96.8	278.3
1135.5	1881.9	280.7			
Alaska		2	10.8	51.6	96.8	284
1331.7	3369.8	753.3			
Arizona		4	9.5	34.2	138.2	312.3
2346.1	4467.4	439.5			

Program using WRAP and NAMED

```
proc report data=sasuser.crime
            wrap        /* wrap lines */
            NAMED       /* prefix values with var=, instead
                           of col. titles */
            nowd ;      * nowd for running in batch ;
   run ;
```

```
State name=Virginia      FIPS code=      51  MURDER=        9
RAPE=      23.3  ROBBERY=    92.1  ASSAULT=    165.7  BURGLARY=     986.2
LARCENY=   2521.2  AUTO=    226.7
State name=Washington    FIPS code=      53  MURDER=      4.3
RAPE=      39.6  ROBBERY=   106.2  ASSAULT=    224.8  BURGLARY=    1605.6
LARCENY=   3386.9  AUTO=    360.3
```

8

Saving space on the page with PROC TABULATE

To get rid of the divider lines in PROC TABULATE output, use the NOSEPS option. To get rid of a line of statistics or labels, specify null labels by using either the KEYLABEL statement or =" against statistics or variables. The RTS (Row Title Space) parameter can be used to control the size of the row title column(s). The RTS value is the width of the columns plus the vertical divider characters. The FORMAT parameter can set the default format for columns (individual column formats may be overridden too). The following is a default PROC TABULATE step followed by a modified PROC TABULATE step

```
proc tabulate data=sasuser.houses ;
   class style bedrooms ;
   var price ;
   table style,
         sum*price*bedrooms ;
```

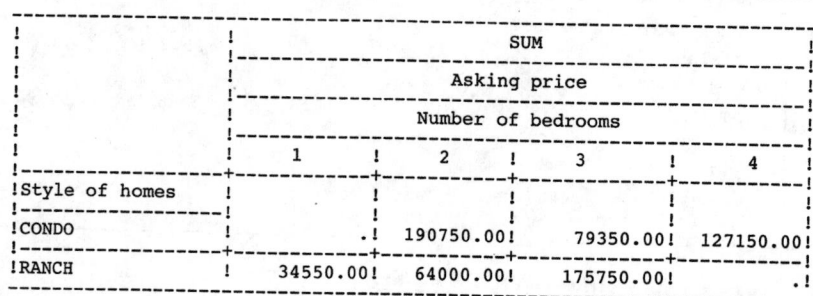

Program with labels set to null and no separator lines

```
proc tabulate data=sasuser.houses
              format=dollar8.
              noseps ;
   class style bedrooms ;
   var price ;
   table style='',
         sum=''*price=''*bedrooms='' /
   rts=10 ;
```

```
 -----------------------------------------------------
 !          !     1    !    2    !    3    !    4    !
 !---------+---------+---------+---------+---------!
 !CONDO    !        .! $190,750! $79,350! $127,150!
 !RANCH    ! $34,550! $64,000! $175,750!        .!
 !SPLIT    ! $65,850!        .! $73,650! $94,450!
 !TWOSTORY!         .! $125,100!        .! $210,200!
 -----------------------------------------------------
```

Defining denominator definitions in PROC TABULATE

Using denominator definitions in PROC TABULATE can be profoundly confusing.

* Remember that you cannot use groupings such as

```
<a*(b c)>
```

but you must show groupings in their ungrouped form. The previous example would then be

```
<a*b a*c>
```

Generally, people want either row or column percentages to add up to 100%.

To get column percentages, specify the ROW definition as the denominator definition:

```
table ROW, column*value*pctn<ROW> ;
```

```
proc tabulate data=sasuser.houses noseps ;
   class style bedrooms ;
   var price ;
   table style, bedrooms*price*pctn<style> ;
run ;
NOTE: The PROCEDURE TABULATE used 0.01 CPU seconds and 1611K.
```

```
-------------------------------------------------------------------
!              !               Number of bedrooms                  !
!              !--------------------------------------------------!
!              !    1    !    2    !    3    !    4    !
!              !---------+---------+---------+---------!
!              !Asking price!Asking price! Asking price! Asking price!
!              !---------+---------+---------+---------!
!              !  PCTN   !  PCTN   !  PCTN   !  PCTN   !
!--------------+---------+---------+---------+---------!
!Style of homes!         !         !         !         !
!CONDO         !         !  40.00! 25.00! 25.00!
!RANCH         !  50.00! 20.00! 50.00!     .!
!SPLIT         !  50.00!     .! 25.00! 25.00!
!TWOSTORY      !     .! 40.00!     .! 50.00!
-------------------------------------------------------------------
```

* To get row percentages, specify the first element of the COLUMN definition as the denominator definition:

```
table row, COLUMN*value*pctn<COLUMN> ;
```

```
    proc tabulate data=sasuser.houses noseps ;
      class style bedrooms ;
      var price ;
      table style, bedrooms*price*pctn<bedrooms> ;
    run ;
NOTE: The PROCEDURE TABULATE used 0.01 CPU seconds and 1611K.
```

```
-----------------------------------------------------------------
!                !                    Number of bedrooms         !
!                !------------------------------------------------!
!                !     1     !     2     !     3     !     4       !
!                !------------------------------------------------!
!                !Asking price !Asking price!Asking price! Asking price!
!                !------------------------------------------------!
!                !    PCTN   !    PCTN   !    PCTN   !    PCTN     !
!----------------+------------------------------------------------!
!Style of homes !           !           !           !             !
!CONDO          !        .! !    50.00! !    25.00! !    25.00!    !
!RANCH          !    25.00! !    25.00! !    50.00! !        .!    !
!SPLIT          !    33.33! !        .! !    33.33! !    33.33!    !
!TWOSTORY       !        .! !    50.00! !        .! !    50.00!    !
-----------------------------------------------------------------
```

For more information

Refer to the *SAS Guide to TABULATE Processing, Second Edition.*

Additional SAS documentation

If you want more information about the tips covered in this section then try reading the relevant SAS documentation.

These manuals include:

- *Reporting from the Field: SAS Software Experts Present Real-World Report-Writing Applications*

- *SAS Language and Procedures: Usage 2, Version 6, First Edition*

Chapter 9
Basic Statistical Procedure Tips

9

FREQ/SUMMARY: frequency tables with long labels

PROC FREQ truncates variable values to 16 characters and then combines identical truncated values. This can give misleading results as in this example.

```
data x ;
  length a $ 30 ;
  input a ;
cards ;
this-is-26-characters-long
this-is-26-characters-long-not
this-is-26-characters-long
run ;

proc freq ;
  table a ;
run ;
```

```
                                               Cumulative  Cumulative
A                     Frequency    Percent    Frequency     Percent
-------------------------------------------------------------------
this-is-26-chara          3         100.0           3        100.0
```

To display full variable values with their frequencies you can use PROC SUMMARY with the NWAY option, followed by PROC PRINT. This does not truncate values.

```
proc summary nway ;
  class a ;
  output out=freq ;
run ;

proc print ;
  var a _freq_ ;
run ;
```

```
OBS                     A                        _FREQ_

 1      this-is-26-characters-long                 2
 2      this-is-26-characters-long-not             1
```

SUMMARY: CLASS versus BY statements

When doing a SUMMARY using a CLASS statement that has variables that have lots of unique values, you may run short of memory. In some cases there is a more efficient way to do the summary.

If you are using PROC SUMMARY on large data sets, consider using PROC SORT and PROC SUMMARY with a BY statement, rather than PROC SUMMARY with a CLASS statement. It seems that a BY statement can be very much more efficient than a CLASS statement.

SAS Institute recommends that the CLASS statement be used instead of the BY statement if there is sufficient memory, as it does use less CPU then a SORT and BY combination. The virtual memory problem occurs because each different instance of the CLASS variable group needs to be stored in virtual memory; therefore, if the number of instances is large, the amount of virtual memory required is also large. This may cause paging problems in a central storage constrained system. My tests show that the CLASS option uses less CPU than SORT and BY in most cases. Of course, if the data is required to be sorted for use in a later process, it may be wiser to use SORT and BY. If the data is already sorted, then CLASS should not be used.

In *SAS Programming Tips: A Guide to Efficient SAS Processing*, tip 8.5 (a CPU tip) states, "Use a CLASS statement in procedures." It goes on to say, "If a procedure supports both the CLASS statement and the BY statement, use the CLASS statement to eliminate the need for sorted input." Rick Aster and Rhena Seidman in *Professional SAS Programming Secrets* strongly recommend the use of CLASS as a programming technique to reduce the number of sorts required. They state that "if you can avoid sorting, by using the SUMMARY procedure, for example, you can make a program run much faster."

I have included part of the output of two jobs that I wrote for test purposes. The first did a SUMMARY with a CLASS statement. The second did a SUMMARY with a BY statement.

First, a part of the job that I used the CLASS statement - this shows that I used 908.49 CPU seconds in doing my SUMMARY with the CLASS statement (before I ran out of memory and the job abended).

```
55      proc sort data=templk.cabsbill nodupkey ;
56      by accno servno month ctotcalr ;
57
58      *;
59      * put data into tape format for sending to a tape on
vik ;
60
61      * summarise to 1 record per account number ;
```

```
NOTE: 500 cylinders dynamically allocated on SYSDA for each of
3 sort work data
NOTE: 33 observations with duplicate key values were deleted.
NOTE: The data set TEMP1K.CABSBILL has 2380144 observations and
13 variables.
NOTE: The PROCEDURE SORT used 41.65 CPU seconds and 62636K.


62      proc summary data=temp1k.cabsbill nway missing ;
63      ***  by accno ; *** try accno on class to compare effi-
ciency ;
64      class accno month icca exch lrd division ;
65      var clocalr cstdr ciddr cmeterr ctotcalr ;
66      output out=work.cabsbill(drop=_type_ rename=(_freq_=ser-
vices))
67      sum= ;
68      run ;

ERROR: PROC SUMMARY was terminated prematurely due to a memory
or disk space shortage
ERROR: PROC SUMMARY was terminated prematurely due to a memory
or disk space shortage
ERROR: PROC SUMMARY was terminated prematurely due to a memory
or disk space shortage
NOTE: The SAS System stopped processing this step because of
insufficient memory
NOTE: SAS set option OBS=0 and will continue to check state-
ments.
WARNING: The data set WORK.CABSBILL may be incomplete.  When
this step was stopped
NOTE: The PROCEDURE SUMMARY used 908.49 CPU seconds and
65110K.
```

Second, here is the job that I put back in that used a SORT followed by a SUMMARY with a BY. This used 126.17 CPU seconds. If you include the SORT, it makes it 169.13 seconds. The SUMMARY with the CLASS took 908.49 before it blew up! That's 739.36 more! That means that the BY method takes less than 20% of the CPU time of the CLASS method (including the SORT).

My theory to explain this is that the CLASS statement with NWAY specified is working out summarization levels for each _TYPE_ value and then is just keeping the top level at the end due to the NWAY. The CLASS statement would also set up tables in memory for keeping all of these stats. Whereas BY just calculates the 'top' level stats.

NOTE: _TYPE_ comes out of the 'BY' method set to 0.

```
57      proc sort data=temp1k.cabsbill nodupkey ;
58      by accno month icca exch lrd division ctotcalr ;
59
60      *;
61      * put data into tape format for sending to a tape on
vik ;
62
63      * summarise to 1 record per account number ;
```

NOTE: 500 cylinders dynamically allocated on SYSDA for each of 3 sort work data
NOTE: 13586 observations with duplicate key values were deleted.
NOTE: The data set TEMP1K.CABSBILL has 2366591 observations and 15 variables.
NOTE: The PROCEDURE SORT used 42.96 CPU seconds and 62632K.

```
64      proc summary data=temp1k.cabsbill nway missing ;
65      by accno month icca exch lrd division ;
66      id accounts ;
67      var clocalr cstdr ciddr cmeterr ctotcalr services ;
68      output out=work.cabsbill(drop=_type_ _freq_)
69      sum= ;
70      run ;
```

NOTE: The data set WORK.CABSBILL has 1842308 observations and 13 variables.
NOTE: The PROCEDURE SUMMARY used 126.17 CPU seconds and 62770K.

MEANS: Specifying confidence limits to calculate

PROC MEANS (which is very similar to PROC SUMMARY) can calculate upper and/or lower confidence limits.

Options on PROC statement, which apply to all variables

ALPHA=*value*   specifies the confidence level as a percentage which is (1-*value*)*100. So by setting ALPHA=0.1, you will get a 90% confidence interval.

CLM   calculates upper and lower confidence limits.

LCLM   calculates lower confidence limit.

UCLM   calculates upper confidence limit.

Keywords for use in OUTPUT statement, which apply to selected variables

Remember to specify the ALPHA= option, even if only using these keywords

LCLM   calculates lower confidence limit.

UCLM   calculates upper confidence limit.

```
      proc means data=sasuser.crime alpha=.05 clm ;
        run ;
      NOTE: The PROCEDURE MEANS used 0.01 CPU seconds and 1419K.
```

```
+---------------------------------------------------------------+
! Variable  Label      Lower 95.0% CLM    Upper 95.0% CLM  !
! --------------------------------------------------------------!
! STATE     FIPS code     24.8347363         33.8052637   !
! MURDER                   6.3450764          8.5429236   !
! RAPE                    22.6761470         28.7918530   !
! ROBBERY                 98.9836150        149.2003850   !
! ASSAULT                182.8083987        239.7916013   !
! BURGLARY                  1169.00            1414.81    !
! LARCENY                   2464.99            2877.59    !
! AUTO                   322.5639147        432.4880853   !
!          --------------------------------------------------- !
+---------------------------------------------------------------+
```

```
      proc summary data=sasuser.crime alpha=.12345 ;
         var assault burglary ;
         output out=bad lclm=low_as low_burg uclm=big_as big_burg
   ;
      run ;
NOTE: The data set WORK.BAD has 1 observations and 6 vari-
ables.
NOTE: The PROCEDURE SUMMARY used 0.01 CPU seconds and 1489K.

      proc print ;
      run ;
NOTE: The PROCEDURE PRINT used 0.00 CPU seconds and 1489K.
```

```
+---------------------------------------------------------------------------+
! OBS    _TYPE_     _FREQ_     LOW_AS     LOW_BURG     BIG_AS     BIG_BURG  !
!                                                                           !
! 1        0          50       189.077    1196.04     233.523    1387.77   !
+---------------------------------------------------------------------------+
```

For more information

See SAS Technical Report P-222, pages 225-226.

UNIVARIATE: mode is the minimum when there are multiples

In PROC UNIVARIATE, the mode of a continuous variable (that is, one with all values unique) is the minimum value in the data set. If there are two or more values the same, then the mode functions correctly. If there are several modes (for example three of two different numbers), then SAS seems to report the smallest mode.

```
data sample ;
   input x ;
cards ;
1
2
3.1
3.5
3.9
4
;
run ;
proc univariate data=sample ;
   var x ;
run ;
```

Output : partial of output from PROC UNIVARIATE

```
Quantiles(Def=5)

   100%  Max        4        99%        4
    75%  Q3       3.9        95%        4
    50%  Med      3.3        90%        4
    25%  Q1         2        10%        1
     0%  Min        1         5%        1
                              1%        1

   Range            3
   Q3-Q1          1.9
   Mode             1
```

UNIVARIATE/FASTCLUS: calculating weighted medians

If the weights are integral, use a FREQ statement instead of a WEIGHT statement with PROC UNIVARIATE.

If the weights are not integral, use PROC FASTCLUS MAXC=1 LEAST=1 in Release 6.07.03 or later to compute an approximate median.

```
data w;
   input x w;
cards;
1  0
3  1
4  2
4  3
7  5
99 10
;

proc univariate;
  var x;
  freq w;
run;

proc fastclus data=w maxc=1 least=1;
  var x;
  weight w;
run;
```

The LEAST=1 option tells FASTCLUS to try to minimize the weighted sum of absolute deviations from the cluster centers. The algorithm is iterative and not exact.

For more information

See *SAS/STAT Software: Changes and Enhancements through Release 6.11*

REG: determining whether to use intercepts

When you are performing a stepwise regression analysis and you are not sure whether you should consider an intercept or not, you can do the following. Create a new variable, INTER, containing the value 1 for each observation and include it in your MODEL statement. This is better than using the default INT option. The stepwise regression methods will show you whether INTER is a variable to take into account or not.

```
data DATASET;
   set DATASET;
   INTER=1;

proc reg data=DATASET;
   model DEP = INDEP1 INDEP2 .. INTER
      / selection=rsquare ...;
run;
```

Additional SAS documentation

If you want more information about the tips covered in this section, then try reading the relevant SAS documentation.

These manuals include:

■ *SAS Language and Procedures: Usage 2, Version 6, First Edition*

9

Chapter 10
The PRINT Procedure

10

A better looking report with BY groups

In a PROC PRINT step, if you specify both an ID and a BY statement that have the same variable names (or lists of variable names), then a special print layout is used. This will also work if the variables in the BY statement are a subset of those in the ID statement. For example, given data which has several observations per subject (SUBJ), then the following code produces the output shown below:

```
proc print;
     ID subj;
     BY subj;
run;
```

```
SUBJ     DAY      VAR1     VAR2     VAR3

001       1        12       34       56
          2        23       45       67
          3        34       56       78

002       1        21       22       23
          2        31       32       33
          3        41       42       43

003       1        10       11       12
```

10

Saving resources by specifying WIDTH

You can save resources in your PROC PRINT step by using WIDTH=FULL. This will use the full width of the format for each column displayed, which means SAS doesn't have to calculate the optimum width for each column. Of course, you may generate more pages this way though. The SAS online Help says:

The WIDTH= option specifies what PROC PRINT uses as the column width when printing the data set. Column width must be one of the following:

FULL   prints the data set using the variable's formatted width as the column width.

MINIMUM|MIN   prints the data set using the minimum column width possible per page to print the data values.

UNIFORM|U   formats all pages uniformly using the variable's formatted width as the column width.

UNIFORMBY|UBY   formats all pages uniformly within a BY group using the variable's formatted width as the column width.

10

Labels are always displayed in BY groups

Here is a very simple thing to watch out for. Everyone knows that the LABEL option in PROC PRINT determines whether variable labels are used for column headings or not. However, variable labels are always used for BY groups (if they are defined). If the BY group variable has no label, or you specify a LABEL VAR='', then the variable name is used. I know of one person that was quite confused since his BY group variable label looked like a list of variable names. The example shows that the BY variable GROUP is displayed in the BY line as its label EXPERIMENTAL GROUP.

```
proc sort data=sasuser.fitness ;
   by group ;
proc print data=sasuser.fitness label ;
   by group ;
   var oxygen runpulse rstpulse ;
run ;
proc print data=sasuser.fitness ;
   by group ;
   var oxygen runpulse rstpulse ;
run ;
```

Output: with LABEL option

```
───────── Experimental group=0 ─────────

                              Heart rate     Heart rate
                 Oxygen          while          while
    OBS       consumption       running        resting

     1          44.609            178            62
     2          45.313            185            62
     3          54.297            156            45
```

Output: without LABEL option

```
───────── Experimental group=0 ─────────

      OBS     OXYGEN     RUNPULSE     RSTPULSE

       1      44.609        178          62
       2      45.313        185          62
       3      54.297        156          45
```

OBS= can't be used in conjunction with a WHERE clause

You cannot use OBS= on a SAS data set when you specify a WHERE clause. This goes for DATA steps and procedures. However, if you put the data set and WHERE clause into a view, then you can use OBS on that view.

Log: Example that fails

```
      proc print data=sasuser.crime(obs=5) ;
         where rape<20 ;
ERROR: A where clause may not be used with the FIRSTOBS or the
OBS data
         set options.
      run;


NOTE: The SAS System stopped processing this step because of
errors.
NOTE: The PROCEDURE PRINT used 0.00 CPU seconds and 1956K.
```

Log: Example that succeeds

```
      data x / view=x ; * Create a view of the SAS dataset ;
        set sasuser.crime ;
           where rape<20 ; * Apply the where clause here ;
      run ;


NOTE: DATA STEP view saved on file WORK.X.
NOTE: The original source statements cannot be retrieved from
a stored
        DATA STEP view nor will a stored DATA STEP view run
under a
        different release of the SAS system or under a different
operating
        system.
        Please be sure to save the source statements for this
DATA STEP
        view.
NOTE: The DATA statement used 0.01 CPU seconds and 1956K.

      proc print data=x(obs=5) ; * Now we can use the OBS parm ;
      run;


NOTE: The view WORK.X.VIEW used 0.01 CPU seconds and 1988K.
NOTE: The PROCEDURE PRINT used 0.01 CPU seconds and 1988K.
```

Additional SAS documentation

If you want more information about the tips covered in this section, then try reading the relevant SAS documentation.

These manuals include:

- *SAS Guide to Report Writing: Examples*
- *SAS Language and Procedures: Usage 2, Version 6, First Edition*

Chapter 11
The FORMAT Procedure

11

Nesting formats within other formats

 From SAS Release 6.07 onwards you can refer to other formats from within formats (value formats not pictures). You can nest your formats up to five levels deep.

```
proc format ;
    value loads
        5000-<6000 = 'Over 5,000'
        6000-<7000 = 'Over 6,000'
        7000-<8000 = 'Over 7,000'
        8000-<9000 = 'Over 8,000'
        other      = 'Mega!' ;
NOTE: Format LOADS has been output.

    value couple
        2 = 'Bingo!'
        5000-<10000 = (!loads10.!)
        other=(!comma6.!) ;
NOTE: Format COUPLE has been output.

NOTE: The PROCEDURE FORMAT used 0.01 CPU seconds and 1480K.

    data _null_ ;
      input x ;
      put x couple. ;
    cards ;
1
2
3
12
1234
5678
8888
9999
12345
;
NOTE: The DATA statement used 0.01 CPU seconds and 1480K.
    run ;
```

```
        1
Bingo!
        3
       12
    1,234
Over 5,000
Over 8,000
Mega!
12,345
```

For more information

See *SAS Technical Report P-222, Changes and Enhancements to Base SAS Software, Release 6.07.*

Modifying standard (in)formats with a custom (in)format

The use of existing formats and informats was covered in a previous tip, but here is a nice application of it.

If your informat or format doesn't do quite what you want, then create a new one based on the original. The new one can handle those special cases that are not handled by the standard one.

The example below shows a DATA step that uses a standard numeric informat to input data that causes errors due to the data having numerics, characters, blanks and missing values. We then make a new informat which handles special values and reads numbers using a standard numeric format.

```
data _null_ ;
   input number 8. ;
   put number= ;
cards ;

NUMBER=10
NUMBER=.
NOTE: Invalid data for NUMBER in line 185 1-8.
NUMBER=.
RULE:—+—1—+—2—+—3—+—4—+—5—+—6—+—
185   PHIL MASON
NUMBER=. _ERROR_=1 _N_=3
NOTE: Invalid data for NUMBER in line 186 1-8.
NUMBER=.
186   sugi 95
NUMBER=. _ERROR_=1 _N_=4
NOTE: The DATA statement used 0.01 CPU seconds and 1530K.


;
run ;
proc format ;
   invalue myfmt
       ' '      = 0
       .        = 0
      'A'-'Z' = 0
      'a'-'z' = 0
       other    = (!8.!) ;
NOTE: Informat MYFMT has been output.
```

NOTE: The PROCEDURE FORMAT used 0.01 CPU seconds and 1530K.

```
data _null_ ;
   input number myfmt. ; * Use our modified informat ;
   put number= ;
cards ;
```

NUMBER=10
NUMBER=0
NUMBER=0
NUMBER=0
NOTE: The DATA statement used 0.01 CPU seconds and 1530K.

```
;
run ; * Now we have no errors !;
* We could set values to a special missing value such as .A
;
   *    which could then be selectively removed ;
```

Mixing character and numeric values in informats

In SAS Release 6.07 onwards, unquoted numerics in INVALUE statements of PROC FORMAT are treated as numbers, whereas they were previously treated as character values. This means that you can now handle character and numeric types with the one informat.

```
proc format ;
   invalue mixed
      1-10  = 1
      11-20 = 2
      'XYZ' = 9
      other=999 ;
run;
```

* In Release 6.06 a value of 111 would be in the 11-20 range and become 2 with this informat.

* In Release 6.07 and higher, 111 falls into the OTHER range and is converted to 999.

For more information

See SAS Technical Report P-222, pages 210, 211, 215 and 216.

Automatically rounding numbers

The ROUND option can be used with PROC FORMAT to display rounded values (Release 6.07 onwards).

This has several advantages:

* avoids doing rounding in a DATA step

* saves on DATA step coding

* retains the precision in the number

* can be used repeatedly in different programs.

In the example below we use a format to display a number in thousands, rounded to the nearest thousand.

```
PROC FORMAT ;
   PICTURE THOU7C (MIN=7 MAX=7 ROUND)
                                  .  = '       O'
      -999999500 <-  -99999500  = '999999' (PREFIX='-'
MULT=.001)
      -99999500  <-< 0           = '00,009' (PREFIX='-'
MULT=.001)
      0             -< 999999500 = '000,009' (MULT=.001)
      OTHER                      = '*******'  ;
NOTE: Format THOU7C has been output.
NOTE: The PROCEDURE FORMAT used 0.01 CPU seconds and 1476K.

data _null_ ;
   format a b c d thou7c. ;
   a=123499.99 ;
   b=123500 ;
   c=-123500 ;
   d=-123499.99 ;
   put _all_ ;
run ;

A=123 B=124 C=-124 D=-123 _ERROR_=0 _N_=1
NOTE: The DATA statement used 0.01 CPU seconds and 1476K.
```

Using long values

Here is something most already know but some don't. Although the online SAS help on PROC FORMAT values says, "These values can be any character string up to forty characters long," from SAS Release 6.07 onwards they can be up to 200 characters.

Example using an 80 character label

```
proc format fmtlib ;
 * Define an 80 character long value ;
value $x
'X' =
'12345678901234567890123456789012345678901234567890aaaaaaaaaabbbbbbbbbbc-
cccccccccddddddddd' ;
NOTE: Format $X has been output.
   run ;

NOTE: The PROCEDURE FORMAT used 0.01 CPU seconds and 1779K.

   data ;
     x='X';
     format x $x. ; * Use the format ;
     put x= ;
   run;

X=12345678901234567890123456789012345678901234567890aaaaaaaaaabbbbbbbbbb-
bccccccccccddddddddd
```

Using formats in a table lookup

SAS programmers often make formats based on SAS data sets, which they then use to lookup or translate data.

How to use a format for lookup

When you want to check whether a value is in a large set of values there are many ways of doing so. Here are the three most obvious ways.

1. Use OR operators, such as

```
if name='fred' or name='john' or name='mike' ;
```

2. Use the IN operator, such as

```
IF name in ('fred','john','mike') ;
```
3. Use a PUT statement with a format, such as

```
IF put(name,$names.)='Y'
```

When you have many values to check against, the statements that use OR and IN operators become difficult to code and rather inefficient to run. The PUT function with a format is quite efficient since formats stay in memory and use binary searching to locate values. Creating the format can be time consuming though. To simplify the task, I have created a macro that generates a format from a SAS data set.

Code Syntax

```
%mkfmt(library.servs,$servs,servno,"Y",other="N",fmtlib=1) ;
```

This creates a format from the SAS data set called LIBRARY.SERVS. The format is called $SERVS. SERVNO is used as the "look-up" value. If found then it returns "Y"; otherwise, it returns "N". I also specified FMTLIB=1 so that my format would be listed after being created. Note that you are required to put quotes around character values for the label and other parameters. This is so that you can alternatively enter numbers if you prefer.

```
%macro mkfmt(dset, fmtname, start, label, other=,
library=library, fmtlib=) ;
%* dset      sas dataset name ;
%* fmtname   name of format to create ;
%* start     variable to be used as START in format ;
%* label     variable to be user for LABEL in format ;
%* other     Optionally set all other values to this variable
or literal;
```

```
%* library   Optionally override default format library to your
own DD ;
%* fmtlib    Put any text here to list your format when created
;

data temptemp(keep=fmtname hlo &start label) ;
   retain fmtname "&fmtname"
   hlo ' ' ;
   set &dset
   end=eofeof ;
   label=&label ; * This could be a variable or a literal ;
   output ;

%if "&other">"" %then
   %do ;
   if eofeof then
      do ;
         hlo='o' ;
         label=&other ;
         output ;
      end ;
%end ;

run ;

proc sort data=temptemp(rename=(&start=start)) nodupkey ;
   by start hlo ;

proc format library=&library
            %if "&fmtlib">"" %then
                fmtlib ;
                cntlin=temptemp ;
            %if "&fmtlib">"" %then
                select &fmtname ; ; * Make sure we only print 1
format from lib ;

run ;

%mend mkfmt ;
```

Additional SAS documentation

If you want more information about the tips covered in this section, then try reading the relevant SAS documentation.

These manuals include:

- *SAS Language and Procedures: Usage 2, Version 6, First Edition*

Chapter 12
SQL

12

Be careful when using SQL

Another view on SQL -

I quote the developer of PROC SQL — "It was really only designed as a user interface tool, not an efficient way to do things in SAS." I heard of one guy who was complaining that SAS on his UNIX machine was hung. Turned out he had left an SQL merge running over the weekend - set it going on Friday, and it was still going on Monday. He didn't know anything about the DATA step, so SAS tech support talked him through the code and then replaced it with a couple of PROC SORT steps followed by a DATA step merge, and the whole job ran - start to finish - in less than 10 minutes!

Many of the problems with PROC SQL arise because of its insistence on forming a Cartesian product and then subsetting based on that. There are, however, other problems - PROC SQL does not optimize as well as a DATA step can if the data sets concerned are pre-sorted or indexed. The advanced programming course contains details of how PROC SQL operates, as well as details about concatenating data sets (PROC APPEND is best, followed closely by a DATA step).

I should, of course, point out that there are some operations for which PROC SQL is invaluable. In particular, fuzzy merges - where, for instance, we have a particular date on one data set, and we want to find a corresponding record on the other which has a start date and an end date. In this case, no exact match is possible, and the DATA step code to do this is complex, to say the least. PROC SQL handles this sort of thing quite elegantly.

I stay clear of SQL unless I have a good reason to use it. My recommendation is that if you are processing large volumes of data, you should also stay clear of it unless absolutely necessary (or unless you have bench marked it thoroughly and are certain that this is one of the rare occasions where SQL out performs the DATA step).

However, SQL is often quick and easy to code. It can be more efficient than equivalent base SAS code. SQL is available in many database systems apart from SAS. For these reasons it is often the best tool to use.

For more information

See *SAS Guide to the SQL Procedure: Usage and Reference, Version 6, First Edition*, pp. 74-78.

Automatic data dictionary information

A wealth of information exists in the SAS online help. One such section relates to SASHELP views and SQL dictionary tables. These are great sources of information about data sets, catalogs, libnames, etc.

PROC SQL dictionary tables are a useful replacement for PROC CONTENTS particularly when you want to get information about data sets into macros. Normally, the dictionary tables can only be accessed under PROC SQL (note dictionary has more than 8 characters) but SAS provides a set of SQL views under the SASHELP libname which allow access from normal DATA steps or procedures (type DIR SASHELP on the command line and you will see what's available). They are excellent for finding out information such as the number of observations in a data set or whether a data set exists or not. This feature only became available under Release 6.07.

Try typing HELP SQL, then select CHANGES & ENHANCEMENTS then NEW SYNTAX then DICTIONARY TABLES then SASHELP VIEWS AND DICTIONARY TABLES then EXAMPLES. This will give you the code and results of about eight pieces of SQL code that use SASHELP views and dictionary tables.

Here's an example (from online help) that shows all the variables in the SAS data set called SQL.EMPLOYE2

```
proc sql;
create view vcol as
select * from dictionary.columns
where libname='SQL' and memname='EMPLOYE2';
NOTE: SQL view USER.VCOL has been defined.
proc print data=vcol label;  run;
```

OBS	LIBNAME	MEMNAME	MEMTYPE	NAME	TYPE
LENGTH ...					
1	SQL	EMPLOYE2	DATA	NAME	char
20					

Here is what the SASHELP VIEWS selection gives you, followed by what the DICTIONARY TABLES selection gives you.

SQL PROCEDURE: SASHELP views

Name of View	*Code which SAS used to create view*
Sashelp.vcatalg	select * from dictionary.catalogs;
Sashelp.vcolumn	select * from dictionary.columns;
Sashelp.vextfl	select * from dictionary.extfiles;
Sashelp.vindex	select * from dictionary.indexes;
Sashelp.vmacro	select * from dictionary.macros;
Sashelp.vmember	select * from dictionary.members;
Sashelp.voption	select * from dictionary.options;
Sashelp.vtable	select * from dictionary.tables;
Sashelp.vtitle	select * from dictionary.titles;
Sashelp.vview	select * from dictionary.views;
Sashelp.vsacces	select libname, memname from dictionary.members where memtype = 'ACCESS' order by libname, memname;
Sashelp.vscatlg	select libname, memname from dictionary.members where memtype = 'CATALOG' order by libname, memname;
Sashelp.vslib	select distinct(libname), path from dictionary.members order by libname;
Sashelp.vstable	select libname, memname from dictionary.members where memtype = 'DATA' order by libname, memname;
Sashelp.vstabvw	select libname, memname, memtype from dictionary.members where memtype in ('VIEW', 'DATA') order by libname, memname;
Sashelp.vsview	select libname, memname from dictionary.members where memtype = 'VIEW';

12

Dictionary.Catalogs

```
DICTIONARY.CATALOGS
    (
    libname  char(8)  label='Library Name',
    memname  char(8)  label='Member Name',
    memtype  char(8)  label='Member Type',
    objname  char(8)  label='Object Name',
    objtype  char(8)  label='Object Type',
    objdesc  char(40) label='Object Description',
    modified char(8)  label='Date Modified',
    alias    char(8)  label='Object Alias'
    );
```

Dictionary.Columns

```
DICTIONARY.COLUMNS
    (
    libname  char(8)  label='Library Name',
    memname  char(8)  label='Member Name',
    memtype  char(8)  label='Member Type',
    name     char(8)  label='Column Name',
    type     char(4)  label='Column Type',
    length   num      label='Column Length',
    npos     num      label='Column Position',
    varnum   num      label='Column Number in Table',
    label    char(40) label='Column Label',
    format   char(16) label='Column Format',
    informat char(16) label='Column Informat',
    idxusage char(9)  label='Column Index Type'
    );
```

Dictionary.Extfiles

```
DICTIONARY.EXTFILES
    (
    FILEREF  char(8)  label='FILEREF',
    xpath    char(80) label='Path Name',
    xengine  char(8)  label='Engine Name'
    );
```

12

Dictionary.Indexes

```
DICTIONARY.INDEXES
   (
    libname   char(8) label='Library Name',
    memname   char(8) label='Member Name',
    memtype   char(8) label='Member Type',
    indxname  char(8) label='Index Name',
    idxusage  char(9) label='Column Index Type',
    name      char(8) label='Column Name',
    indxpos   num     label='Position of Column in Concatenated
Key',
    nomiss    char(3) label='Nomiss Option',
    unique    char(3) label='Unique Option'
   );
```

Dictionary.Macros - new to SAS 6.11

```
DICTIONARY.MACROS
   (
    SCOPE      char(9)   label='Macro Scope',
    NAME       char(8)   label='Macro Variable Name',
    OFFSET     num       label='Offset into Macro Variable',
    VALUE      char(200) label='Macro Variable Value'
   );
```

Dictionary.Members

```
DICTIONARY.MEMBERS
   (
    libname   char(8)  label='Library Name',
    memname   char(8)  label='Member Name',
    memtype   char(8)  label='Member Type',
    engine    char(8)  label='Engine Name',
    index     char(8)  label='Indexes',
    path      char(80) label='Path Name'
   );
```

Dictionary.Options

```
DICTIONARY.OPTIONS
   (
    optname   char(20)  label='Session Option Name',
    setting   char(200) label='Session Option Setting',
    optdesc   char(80)  label='Option Description'
   );
```

12

Dictionary.Tables

```
DICTIONARY.TABLES
   (
      libname   char(8)   label='Library Name',
      memname   char(8)   label='Member Name',
      memtype   char(8)   label='Member Type',
      memlabel  char(40)  label='Dataset Label',
      typemem   char(8)   label='Dataset Type',
      crdate    num       format=datetime14. label='Date Created',
      modate    num       format=datetime14. label='Date
Modified',
      nobs      num       label='Number of Observations',
      obslen    num       label='Observation Length',
      nvar      num       label='Number of Variables',
      protect   char(3)   label='Type of Password Protection',
      compress  char(8)   label='Compression Routine',
      reuse     char(3)   label='Reuse Space',
      bufsize   num       label='Bufsize',
      delobs    num       label='Number of Deleted Observations',
      indxtype  char(9)   label='Type of Indexes'
   );
```

Dictionary.Titles - new to SAS 6.11

```
DICTIONARY.TITLES
   (
     TYPE      char(1)    label='Title Location',
     NUMBER    num        label='Title Number',
     TEXT      char(200)  label='Title Text'
   );
```

Dictionary.Views

```
DICTIONARY.VIEWS
   (
      libname char(8) label='Library Name',
      memname char(8) label='Member Name',
      memtype char(8) label='Member Type',
      engine  char(8) label='Engine Name'
   );
```

Conditional arithmetic

The SUM function is a standard SQL function; however, it has some extended uses when used in conjunction with other functions.

```
Select
  SUM (CASE FRED
           WHEN 'A' THEN AMOUNT
                         ELSE 0
       END) AS FREDAMT
  From data.set ;
```

This would cause the output variable FREDAMT to contain only the sum of the FRED 'A' records. SUM can also be used to sum across the columns in a row, for example, SUM (A, B, C). Be very careful when using it in this form as a performance bottleneck has been discovered in the case where A, B and C contain missing values. If your data has a high proportion of missing values and if it is not required to distinguish between zero and missing, consider setting missing values to zero prior to such a function.

12

Providing values to use in place of missing values

In PROC SQL the COALESCE function can be used to set default values when variables have missing values. The COALESCE function is almost essential when doing left, right or full joins where the key fields are included in the output set only once.

To replace missing values of VAR1 from data set X, with values of VAR1 from Y,

select var2 as in this example:

```
coalesce(x.var1, y.var1) as var1
from y left join x
on x.var2=y.var2 ;
```

For more information

See the example on page 73 of the *SAS Guide to the SQL Procedure: Usage and Reference, Version 6, First Edition.*

12

Using values just calculated

From Release 6.07 on, you can use the CALCULATED keyword in SAS SQL to use values calculated in an SQL statement elsewhere in that statement. This avoids the need to recalculate the values, thereby saving resources.

The following example avoids recalculating the value for use in the WHERE clause.

```
proc sql ;
   select style,
          bedrooms,
          price/sqfeet as value
   from sasuser.houses
   where calculated value > 55 ;
```

Examining resource usage in SQL

When you use SQL code that has more than one statement per PROC SQL step, the resource usage stats for each statement are combined to give a total at the end of the PROC. This is the default action since it takes SAS less resources to do this than to keep track of resource usage for each SQL statement.

If you are tuning your code and want to get the resource usage for each SQL statement, then you should specify the RESET STIMER statement. This will then give the resources for each SQL statement. This gives you some more insight into the performance of your code.

The example below shows two PROC SQL steps with identical SQL statements. The second has RESET STIMER specified.

```
2        proc sql ;
3        select * from sasuser.class where sex='F' ;
4        select * from sasuser.class where age>15 ;
NOTE: The PROCEDURE SQL used 0.03 CPU seconds and 1816K.
5        proc sql ;
6        reset stimer ;
NOTE: The SQL Statement used 0.00 CPU seconds and 1816K.
7        select * from sasuser.class where sex='F' ;
NOTE: The SQL Statement used 0.01 CPU seconds and 1816K.
8        select * from sasuser.class where age>15 ;
NOTE: The SQL Statement used 0.01 CPU seconds and 1816K.
```

Generating statements to define data set/view structure

As an alternative to PROC CONTENTS or PROC DATASETS, you could use SQL to see the structure of a SAS data set or view. Use:

```
DESCRIBE VIEW view-name
```

or

```
DESCRIBE TABLE table-name
```

The output (which goes to the LOG) could then be copied in order to create a new data set or view.

```
    proc sql ;
        describe table sasuser.fitness ;

NOTE: SQL table SASUSER.FITNESS was created like:

create table SASUSER.FITNESS( label='Exercise/fitness study
data set' bufsize=6144 )
  (
   AGE num label='Age in years',
   WEIGHT num label='Weight in kg',
   RUNTIME num label='Min. to run 1.5 miles',
   RSTPULSE num label='Heart rate while resting',
   RUNPULSE num label='Heart rate while running',
   MAXPULSE num label='Maximum heart rate',
   OXYGEN num label='Oxygen consumption',
   GROUP num label='Experimental group'
  );
```

12

Submit SQL works with TESTAF

You may think that you can test any application using TESTAF; however, some cannot be properly tested.

SUBMIT SQL blocks in SAS/AF code execute properly using TESTAF; however, other SUBMIT blocks do not. To execute other submit blocks you must leave the BUILD procedure and run the application.

Additional SAS documentation

If you want more information about the tips covered in this section, then try reading the relevant SAS documentation.

These manuals include:

- *SAS Guide to the SQL Procedure: Usage and Reference, Version 6, First Edition*
- *Getting Started with the SQL Procedure, Version 6, First Edition*

12

Chapter 13
SCL

13

Making methods memory resident

There is a feature in SCL that allows you to make your SCL methods memory resident in much the same way that you make your SAS/AF PROGRAM entries resident. All you need to do is to specify the RESIDENT option when defining your method.

If you expect to use one or more methods frequently during a session, then your application performance may be improved by using the RESIDENT or NOINITIAL options.

When the RESIDENT option is used, all methods in an SCL entry will be held resident in memory after one of the methods has executed.

```
prodcode:
method dataprof 8 prodcode $ / resident ;
prodcode=getnitemc(dataprof,'prodcode') ; endmethod;
```

This method is called PRODCODE, it has two parameters defined and it is resident in memory. This not only reduces the response time but may even reduce the number of I/Os (as we found in our case).

Some people have had some slight trouble using this option. One person had 10 methods in the same SCL entry and had the RESIDENT option on only some of them. This should cause all the methods in any one SCL entry to become resident. However, the methods could often crash when calling each other until they are all given the RESIDENT option. (It is best to put the RESIDENT option in a macro variable so it is easy to switch on and off and compare the different performance- it does make a difference.)

The NOINITIAL option is similar to the RESIDENT option except that the SCL vector is not automatically initialized to missing when a method is called. This could improve performance further, although you will need to handle variable initialization in your SCL code. The NOINTIAL option is a Release 6.11 feature.

For more information

See *SAS/AF Software: FRAME Entry Usage and Reference*, page 115.

Variable names and list item names in SCL can be long

In SCL variable names can be up to 32 characters long. SCL list-item names can be 200 characters long.

```
init:
  list=makelist() ;
  x100=repeat('—+—!',10) ; * 100 character long string ;
  list=setnitemc(list,'Value',x100!!x100!!x100) ; * try for 300
chars ;
  call putlist(list,'List') ;
  this_is_a_very_long_variable='So it is!' ;
  this_is_a_very_long_variable_2_____='They can be 32
char!!!' ;
  put _all_ ;
return ;
```

```
NOTE: Compiling VARLEN.SCL.
WARNING: [Line 7]  Variable name THIS_IS_A_VERY_LONG_VARI-
ABLE_2_____ is too long. Only
          the first 32 characters will be applied.
WARNING: [Line 6]  Variable THIS_IS_A_VERY_LONG_VARIABLE is
defined but not used
WARNING: [Line 7]  Variable THIS_IS_A_VERY_LONG_VARIABLE_2__ is
defined but not used

NOTE: Code generated for VARLEN.SCL. Code size=660.
List(—+—!—+—!—+—!—+—!—+—!—+—!—+—!—+—!—+—!—+—
-!—+—!—+—!—+—!—+—!—+—!—+—!—+—!—+—!—+—!
—+—!—+—!='Value' )[5]
LIST = 5
THIS_IS_A_VERY_LONG_VARIABLE = 'So it is!'
THIS_IS_A_VERY_LONG_VARIABLE_2__ = 'They can be 32 char!!!'
X100 =
'—+—!—+—!—+—!—+—!—+—!—+—!—+—!—+—!—+—!—
—+—!—+—!'
_CURROW_ = .
_ERROR_ = .
_MSG_ = ''
_STATUS_ = ' '
```

13

Using environment lists to pass information

Local

In SCL each SAS System application (such as an FSEDIT application or any application started with the AF or AFA commands) has a unique local environment list. This enables data to be shared between programs within that application. The list-id for the local environment list can be obtained using: *list-id*=ENVLIST('L') ; One application's local environment list *cannot* be accessed from a different application.

Global

The global environment list can be used to share data across all SAS applications in one SAS session. Use: *list-id*=ENVLIST('G') ; to get its list identifier.

Tips

1. Rather than passing entry parameters between programs, you can put parameters on the local environment list.

2. Parameters unique to a SAS session (for example, printer id, user details, etc.) can be placed on the global environment list and then are available for any application to use.

3. You can put user preferences for an application into a list on the local environment list. This can then be saved at the end of the application and loaded at the start of the application. This means that your application will remember the users' preferences. The same goes for saving the global environment list to load/save SAS session parameters.

13

Displaying a CATALOG selection list

The feature of the CATLIST SCL function described here is undocumented prior to SAS Release 6.11. It is, however, documented and supported in SAS Release 6.11.

```
names = catlist('*', <other parameters the same...> );
```

Prior to Release 6.08, you had to specify a catalog name as the first parameter. With the new function, you can put a '*' in and you'll get the three-listbox window to make your selections.

The '*' option is available in Release 6.08, although it seems that the number of selections is ignored. That is, if you tell it three maximum selections, it lets you select as many as you want.

Also, it does not pre-select anything like the 'regular' CATLIST function does.

For more information

See *SAS Screen Control Language: Reference*, pages 249-250.

Determining or causing an END or CANCEL

The _STATUS_ variable in SCL can be used to determine if a user entered an END or CANCEL or to tell SAS to resume execution of a program or stop execution of a program. It is valuable in modifying the flow of your program and especially in handling errors.

You can check the SCL _STATUS_ system variable value for these conditions:

STATUS='E'   user entered an END command.

STATUS='C'   user entered a CANCEL command.

You may also set the value of _STATUS_ to force SAS to take the following actions:

STATUS='R'   Resume execution of the SCL program. Set this value in the TERM section so that after a user issues an END or CANCEL, the SCL will resume execution

STATUS='H'   Stop execution of the current SCL program on encountering the next RETURN statement. If you want your program to end immediately; then code a RETURN directly after _STATUS_='H'.

STATUS has several more values for FRAME entries.

'P'   A pop-up menu event occurred.

'G'   The GETROW section was called for the top row of an extended table.

'K'   A command other than an END or CANCEL, or their equivalents, was issued.

'D'   A widget was selected with a double click.

' '   A widget has been selected or modified.

Notes:

STATUS='R'   This doesn't have to be set in the TERM section; it can be set anywhere in any section. This is important to remember because you don't always have to have a TERM section (though it's good practice to have one). For example, in a FRAME entry an object's label will execute if the 'END' or 'CANCEL' command is executed while that widget has the focus.

STATUS='H'   This will only take effect at the end of INIT, MAIN and TERM sections, that is, when return is passed back to the screen. Setting _STATUS_='H' in another section will not cause the program to stop and go back to its caller. In order to get the program entry to halt immediately, you need to code a STOP; statement before the RETURN; statement.

13

SCL Code

```
init:
   link test ;
   put 'in init after test' ;
return ;

main:
return ;

term:
return ;

test:
  put 'in test' ;
  _STATUS_ = 'H' ;
return ;
```

The previous code would result in the following output in the MSG or LOG window:

```
in test
in init after test
```

If we recode the TEST section as follows:

```
test:
  put 'in test' ;
  _STATUS_ = 'H' ;
  stop ;
return ;
```

The output in the MSG or LOG window would now be

```
in test
```

For more information

See *SAS Screen Control Language: Reference, Version 6, First Edition*, page 18.

SCL function to calculate statistics from a data set

The SCL function, VARSTAT, is used to calculate simple statistics for SAS data set variables. The syntax for the VARSTAT function is

```
rc=VARSTAT(data-set-id,varlist-1,statistics,varlist-2) ;
```

Often VARSTAT can be used in place of PROC SUMMARY or SQL to get statistics from a data set. The VARSTAT function often runs much quicker than these other facilities. To do a SUMMARY or SQL (from AF) you must use a SUBMIT CONTINUE and then the code is interpreted by SAS, whereas SCL code is compiled.

In SAS Release 6.08 the performance of the VARSTAT command was significantly improved for large data sets. It is now suitable for using on all sizes of data sets. Also, several other statistics were supported: median, mode, kurtosis and skewness.

In the following example, we have the code for producing some statistics from a data set in three different ways.

SCL VARSTAT

```
dsid=open('sasuser.crime') ;
rc=varstat(dsid,'murder,rape','std
mean',stdmurd,avgmurd,stdrape,avgrape) ;
rc=close(dsid) ;
```

PROC MEANS or PROC SUMMARY

```
26    proc means data=sasuser.crime nway ;
27      var murder rape ;
28      output out=temp
29            std(murder rape)=
30            mean(murder rape)=avgmurd avgrape ;
```

```
NOTE: The data set WORK.TEMP has 1 observations and 6 vari-
ables.
NOTE: The PROCEDURE MEANS used 0.01 CPU seconds and 1980K.
```

PROC SQL

```
31    proc sql ;
32      select
33        std(murder) AS murder,
34        std(rape) AS rape,
35        mean(murder) AS avgmurd,
36        mean(rape) AS avgrape
37      FROM sasuser.crime ;
38    quit ;
NOTE: The PROCEDURE SQL used 0.02 CPU seconds and 1980K.
```

13

Using macros in SCL

By using macros for common and repetitive programming tasks, you can save a lot of time when coding SCL. However, be aware that the macros invoked are resolved when the SCL program is compiled. This is one reason why it is usually better to use SCL methods than macros.

Additionally, any macro variables referenced use the values assigned at compile time NOT at run time. Make sure any macro variables being used have values assigned at compile time, if needed. If you want to deal with macro variables at run time, then use the SYMGET and SYMPUT functions.

Debugging SCL using environment-dependent macros

Debugging SCL can be made easier by defining an autocall macro to write out data. This is called at compile time, which allows for different behavior in different environments.

Development   macro contains debugging commands.

Production   macro resolves without generating any code, so production compile does not contain the debugging commands.

Using this method, it is possible to change the behavior of the SCL without actually altering the code. Changing the macro and compiling is all that is required to enable/disable the debugging. If the development and production macros are kept in separate libraries (for example, MVS -> PDS, DOS -> Directory) then the change from development to production can be parameterized. An example follows.

```
Development Macro:
  00001 %macro trace(parms);
  00002    %* Trace macro ;
  00003
  00004    put &parms;
  00005
  00006 %mend;
Production Macro:
  00001 %macro trace(parms);
  00002    %* Trace macro ;
  00003
  00004    %* &parms;
  00005
  00006 %mend;

SCL:
  00120 WHERE:
  00121    method where_in $200;
  00122      where=where_in;
  00123      link open;
  00124      if rc=0
  00125      then
  00126         link getvars;
  00127      link close;
  00128
  00129      %trace('WHERE:' where= rc= msg=);
  00130    endmethod;
```

Arrays can be passed by reference in Release 6.11

In SAS Release 6.11 (SAS/AF) arrays can be passed by reference without the need to define the array in both the calling and called program. This requires far less memory than previously, since arrays only exist once in memory yet can be used by multiple programs.

Refaray1.scl

```
init:
 ** Define an array to be passed to another SCL program ;
  array temp(6) $ 10 ('January' 'February' 'March' 'April'
'May' 'June') ;
  put _all_ ; ** Show contents of the array ;
  call display('refaray2.scl',temp) ; * Passing an array by
reference ;
  return ;
```

Refaray2.scl

```
array passed(*) $ ; ** Let the SCL know that an array is being
passed ;
entry passed $ ; ** Define what to call it in this program ;
init:
  put 'Now in called SCL program: refaray2' ;
  put _all_ ; ** Show that the array has been successfully
passed ;
  return ;
```

```
TEMP[1] = 'January'
TEMP[2] = 'February'
TEMP[3] = 'March'
TEMP[4] = 'April'
TEMP[5] = 'May'
TEMP[6] = 'June'
_CURROW_ = .
_ERROR_ = .
_MSG_ = ''
_STATUS_ = ' '
```

Now in called SCL program: refaray2

```
PASSED[1] = 'January'
PASSED[2] = 'February'
PASSED[3] = 'March'
PASSED[4] = 'April'
PASSED[5] = 'May'
PASSED[6] = 'June'
_CURROW_ = .
_ERROR_  = .
_MSG_    = ''
_STATUS_ = ' '
```

For more information

See *SAS Screen Control Language: Reference, Version 6, Second Edition*, page 232 and following.

Open data sets for sequential input to improve performance

If you only require sequential access to a data set, then you can improve your program's performance by specifying the 'IS' pattern in the SCL OPEN function. This opens the data set for input, sequential read.

```
data-set-id=OPEN(<data-set-name>,'IS') ;
```

Another obvious improvement can be made by the use of WHERE functions to reduce the number of observations read. It is also useful to cut down the number of variables in the data set being read. The fewer variables, the smaller the data, the less I/O, the quicker your program runs.

13

Delete lists to save memory

When using SCL, you should delete lists when they are no longer needed or else they will remain in memory (taking up valuable memory) until the application (not the program) in which they were created ends.

```
rc=DELLIST(list-id) ;
```

If using sublists, then you should use an extra parameter on the DELLIST command which will delete each sublist on the list (including each of its sublists).

```
rc=DELLIST(list-id,'Y') ;
```

If you don't delete sublists recursively, then any sublists will remain in memory. Make sure you keep their list-id on another list or in an SCL variable; otherwise, you will have no way of using (or deleting) them.

Note: Of course, you can't delete the local or global environment lists.

For more information

See SAS Technical Report P-216, pages 145-146.

How to test SUBMIT blocks in SAS/AF

You can use TESTAF to test SUBMIT SQL blocks in your SCL, but you cannot do the same with other SUBMIT blocks in SCL (ie. non-SQL). This can be a problem when debugging programs. However, you can test/debug SUBMIT blocks in AF by compiling the AF entry with DEBUG ON while in BUILD, then save the FRAME entry and enter:

```
DM 'AF C=libref.catalog DEBUG=YES' AF:
```

You then get put into the SCL debugger, but like looking at SUBMIT SQL in the debugger, you don't get to see the processing of the SUBMIT block. This can be seen by invoking the DATA step debugger from within your SUBMIT block.

Another useful way to test the code inside SUBMIT blocks is to take the code out and run it on its own from the PROGRAM EDITOR. Once it is tested, it can be put back in the SUB-MIT block. Remember that you can use the DATA step debugger for debugging DATA steps.

13

Replacing SCL variable values in SUBMIT blocks

Syntax: REPLACE *variable 'replacement-string'*;

The REPLACE statement (non-executable) replaces the current value of an SCL variable with a replacement string in the SUBMIT block. The replacement occurs only if the SCL variable is not blank. The replacement string can reference other SCL variables.

The following SCL example would write out "My name is Phil Mason".

```
name='Phil' ;
replace name 'My name is &name Mason' ;
submit ;
  %put &name ;
endsubmit;
```

For more information

See *SAS Screen Control Language: Reference, Version 6, First Edition*, pages 54-55.

Use same case in SCL constants

Constants defined in SCL are stored in the compiled code. Each time the code runs, the data is loaded, so the data should be as small as possible to reduce storage and I/O time.

Reducing the number of constants will reduce the size of the code. Reducing the case variations of constants will reduce the size of the code also since only one copy of each constant is stored.

It is useful to adopt a standard such as:

All constants should be kept in uppercase unless comparing with data in mixed case.

In the example that follows, example 2 compiles to a smaller size since only one copy of the data set name is stored.

```
1 -- if ... the call fsedit('sasuser.crime') ; else call
fsbrowse('SASUSER.CRIME') ;

2 -- if ... the call fsedit('SASUSER.CRIME') ; else call
fsbrowse('SASUSER.CRIME') ;
```

13

Remote command determines where SUBMIT blocks run

When using SAS/CONNECT and using submit blocks in SCL, you can issue the REMOTE command to toggle whether code from SUBMIT blocks will be remotely or locally submitted by default.

Command	Action
REMOTE	toggle remote/local submit from SCL submit blocks
REMOTE ON	submit blocks will remote submit
REMOTE OFF	submit blocks will local submit

NOTE: Specifying the REMOTE keyword on the SUBMIT block overrides the default setting.

This feature can be used in conjunction with SAS/ASSIST to cause generated code to be executed remotely. Keep a small (0 or 1 obs) copy of the remote data set locally to allow SAS/ASSIST to build its code based on that. Allocate a LIBNAME with the same libref on local and remote host. That means that when you submit remotely, the code generated locally will execute without change.

13

Saving and retrieving parameters in PROGRAM entries

You can use Call SAVESCREEN() to save all parameters on a PROGRAM entry when in use. The parameters can then be recalled when starting the application by using AUTORE-CALL=YES on the AF command.

13

Getting SCL help online in Windows

If you are developing using FRAME and SCL (in Windows), there actually is some online help available that's really useful. A Windows help database is provided in Release 6.10 and higher that documents all of the "important" SCL functions and most of the Frame widgets (methods and all). By setting up a little AF application to start the Windows help engine, you can effectively get most of the information from *SAS Screen Control Language: Reference* and *SAS/AF Software: FRAME Entry, Usage and Reference* online.

How To Get into the Help File

The help database file is: \SAS\CORE\WINHELP\FSP.HLP. You can peruse this file by just using the OPEN function in the WINHELP program. (WINHELP is started by entering "WINHELP" at any Windows RUN prompt). But to make this easier, you can use the following SCL program:

```
init:
    rc=winhelp('help_contents','c:\sas\core\winhelp\fsp.hlp');
    return;
```

(The WINHELP SCL function just kicks off WINHELP.) Now, to make this really slick, you can define either a function key or a toolbar button to run the program. Assuming you saved the above program as CALLHELP.SCL in a catalog called TOOLS in the libref MYTOOLS, the command to run it would be:

```
afa c=MYTOOLS.TOOLS.callhelp.scl
```

(Note: AFA is used instead of AF so you can run this at the same time as another AF application.)

Finding What You Want in the Help File

There is a lot of information in this help file, but the two most useful pages I have found yet are called:

SAS/AF FRAME Entry - lists the FRAME Widgets, etc.

SCL: SCL Elements - lists SCL functions, language elements

Getting to these pages can be a real pain by navigating through all the hot-links in the file. Once I found them, I saved them as bookmarks, so that now they are available from the BOOKMARKS pull-down when I first get in the help file. (Defining a bookmark just means going to the page you want and clicking on the Define... item under the BOOK-MARKS pull-down).

13

To find these two pages, just follow the (little green) links:

For SAS/AF FRAME Entry:

Introduction -> FRAME -> Available Classes Of Objects ->

For SCL: SCL Elements:

Introduction -> SCL -> SCL -> Syntax -> SCL Elements ->

For people who don't want to carry manuals around, this is a real time-saver. I'm not sure how this applies on other operating systems (UNIX, OS/2), but I'll bet there is something similar.

13

Additional SAS documentation

If you want more information about the tips covered in this section, then try reading the relevant SAS documentation.

These manuals include:

- SAS Applications Programming: A Gentle Introduction
- SAS Screen Control Language: Reference, Version 6, Second Edition
- SAS/AF Software: FRAME Application Development Concepts, Version 6, First Edition
- SAS/AF Software: FRAME Class Dictionary, Version 6, First Edition
- Beyond the Obvious with SAS Screen Control Language
- Professional SAS User Interfaces

13

Chapter 14
FRAME Entries

14

Using different cursor shapes for different objects

By using the _SET_CURSOR_SHAPE_ method, you can tell SAS what shape the mouse pointer should take when moving over a widget in a frame (SAS Release 6.10 & 6.11). This seems to be undocumented prior to Release 6.11.

To try out cursor shapes, make 20 widgets in a frame (for example, pushbuttons). As you make them, they will be automatically named OBJ1 to OBJ20. Then copy the following code into the source window. Compile it. TESTAF it. Now you can see the mouse pointer change shape as it moves over each of the widgets.

```
init:
    call notify('obj1','_set_cursor_shape_',1) ; * Hourglass ;
    call notify('obj2','_set_cursor_shape_',2) ; * Arrow ;
    call notify('obj3','_set_cursor_shape_',3) ; * Cross-hair ;
    call notify('obj4','_set_cursor_shape_',4) ; * Medium
Magnifying glass ;
    call notify('obj5','_set_cursor_shape_',5) ; * Hand ;
    call notify('obj6','_set_cursor_shape_',6) ; * Copy ;
    call notify('obj7','_set_cursor_shape_',7) ; * Question mark
;
    call notify('obj8','_set_cursor_shape_',8) ; * Small
Magnifying glass ;
    call notify('obj9','_set_cursor_shape_',9) ; * Big Magnifying
glass ;
    call notify('obj10','_set_cursor_shape_',10) ; * Horizontal
double arrow ;
    call notify('obj11','_set_cursor_shape_',11) ; * Vertical
double arrow ;
    call notify('obj12','_set_cursor_shape_',12) ; * 4-way arrow
;
    call notify('obj13','_set_cursor_shape_',13) ; * TopLeft to
BottomRight 2x arrow ;
    call notify('obj14','_set_cursor_shape_',14) ; * BottomLeft
to TopRight 2x arrow ;
    call notify('obj15','_set_cursor_shape_',15) ; * Screen ;
    call notify('obj16','_set_cursor_shape_',16) ; * 3 charts ;
    call notify('obj17','_set_cursor_shape_',17) ; * OK ;
    call notify('obj18','_set_cursor_shape_',18) ; * Dont ;
    call notify('obj19','_set_cursor_shape_',19) ; * Pointer with
a question mark ;
    call notify('obj20','_set_cursor_shape_',0) ;  * Vertical
cursor ;
return ;
```

14

In Release 6.10 cursor shapes are not documented, which means they are not supported, although they do actually work. They are documented in Release 6.11.

To further test the cursor shapes, make a slider or scrollbar (called SBAR). Set the MIN to 0 and the MAX to 19. Make a text entry field (called TEXT) and use the following code:

```
sbar: call notify( 'sbar', '_set_cursor_shape_', sbar );
      text=sbar ;
return;
```

You can also set the cursor shape on the frame itself.

```
init: call notify( '.', '_set_cursor_shape_', number );
```

Displaying a file selection list

Among the many undocumented features of Release 6.10 is the FILEDIALOG SCL function (which has completely different syntax from Release 6.11).

Release 6.10 Syntax

```
filename = filedialog('open') ;
```

which returns in the variable FILENAME a file selected from the dialog that gets popped up. This is useful in a Release 6.10 application, no obvious problems with it, just a totally different syntax from Release 6.11. This has been tested and works in OS/2 and Windows.

Release 6.11 Syntax

```
rc =filedialog(dialog_type,filename<,default-file<,default-
dir<list of filters.....
```

The details are in *SAS Screen Control Language: Reference, Version 6, Second Edition*. It certainly works in Release 6.10 as above, but the above syntax change is enough to ensure that anyone using Release 6.10 must change code before they use Release 6.11.

This is an UNDOCUMENTED feature and therefore is an UNSUPPORTED feature. So if you are worried about support, then don't use undocumented features.

14

Programming a delay

The SCL function rc=SLEEP(n); will tell SAS to 'sleep' or suspend execution for the time specified in n (seconds). When the SLEEP function is operating, a pop-up window appears telling you how long the SAS System is going to sleep. If you are using this function in an AF application, the pop-up window may be undesirable. There is no documented way of switching this window off. However, the MCIPISLP function can provide the same delay functionality as the SLEEP function without displaying a pop-up window.

The function syntax is:

```
rc=MCIPISLP(n);
```

where n is the time in seconds.

Note that both functions are system dependent.

14

Automatically loading a default SCL template when creating a new FRAME entry

Most sites will have programming standards in place. Often program templates are used for completely new programs. These templates may contain a standard comment block at the head of the program stating the purpose of the program, author, modifications etc. When a new SCL entry is created, an SCL template can be manually loaded by copying the template in (for example, in the SCL window issuing the command: COPY TEMPLATE.SCL where TEMPLATE.SCL is the place where the template is stored in the current catalog). Alternatively, if you want to do this automatically when the FRAME entry is created, you can subclass the FRAME class:

1. Create a new class, specifying the parent class as SASHELP.FSP.FRAME.

2. Create an instance variable (char, non automatic) called SCL_TEMPLATE, having the value of the SCL catalog entry that is to be used as the SCL template.

3. Override the _BPOSTINIT_ method with the method listed below (as BPOST).

4. Compile and save the overwritten method.

5. Enter the new FRAME class in the resource entry.

6. In the resource entry, select the new FRAME class and set this to active (under actions).

```
/*Methods for Sunken Treasure Software Systems Ltd Frame Class
   Written by Mark Bodt 28 March 1996 */

length frame scl classname $35 catname $17;

*avoid compile time warnings;
 _self_ = _self_;
 rc=rc;
 classname=classname;


BPOST    : method;
/* Create an SCL program for the frame */


    /* Create name for SCL entry to be copied            */

      *get the name of the new frame;
       call send(_self_,'_GET_NAME_',frame);
```

14

```
      *get the library and catalog of the SCL template;
       /* this will be in the same catalog as the class
          therefore we will find out the class name and
          extract the library and catalog names */
          call send(_self_,'_GET_CLASS_',classid);
          call send(classid,'_GET_NAME_',classname);
          catname=scan(classname,1,'.')||'.'||scan(class-
name,2,'.');

      *assemble new SCL entry name;
       scl_template=getnitemc(_self_,'SCL_TEMPLATE');
       scl_template=compress(catname||'.'||scl_template);

      *assemble new SCL entry name- Strip off FRAME and add
SCL;
       scl=substr(frame,1,length(frame)-5)||'SCL';

      /*if the SCL entry does not exist then create it based on
        the SCL template. */
      if not cexist(scl) then do;
       rc=copy(scl_template,scl,'CATALOG');
       if rc ne 0 then do;*copy failed - error handling;
         sysmsg=sysmsg();
         put 'ERROR: New SCL entry ' scl
         ' could not be created.';
         put '        The system message was: ' sysmsg;
         alarm;
        end;*copy failed - error handling;
       else do;
         *rename SCL entry description;
         scl1=scan(scl,3,'.');/*get one level name*/
         rc=rename(scl,scl1,'CATALOG','SCL entry for '||
             scan(frame,3,'.')||'.FRAME');
        end;
      end; *create SCL entry;

  *call parent class method;
    call super(_self_,'_bpostinit_');
endmethod;
```

Specifying automatic filter lists for Open and Save As

When using SAS Release 6.10 under Windows you can make use of the FILE OPEN and FILE SAVE AS dialogs together with a filter to display only files matching your definition. The following usage note tells you how.

Usage Note:

```
V6-SYS.DMS-9462                              USAGE NOTE

File Open Filter list is available but undocumented in 6.10

Product:  BASE

If you want to change the default filter list for the File
Open and File Save As dialog boxes you can use an undocumented
dollar ($) option in the config.sas. For example if you want
to have the List of File Type: section of the dialog boxes
default to *.* followed by *.txt you would put $filterlist
"*.* *.txt" in the config.sas file.

As an alternative, a toolbar icon can be set up with a Command
of
   dlgopen filter='*.* *.txt'.

   If you use both at the same time, make sure that the $fil-
terlist option in the CONFIG.SAS file has double quotes around
the filters.  If you use single quotes around the $filterlist
option you will encounter:

         Error: Access Violation (80000602)
                   Ok

         Error: A severe error occurred in task PROGRAM for mod-
ule
         SASVWU executing in module SASVWU at address 00023F78
                                     Ok

SAS Note Revised On:   20OCT94

System     Release Reported   Release Fixed

Windows    6.10   TS019

No Zaps Available
```

14

Tabbing to non-text fields in a frame on the Windows platform

The TAB key on the Windows platform behaves differently for the character-based objects than it does for the pixel-based objects. For Releases 6.10 and 6.11, the PC host takes over tabbing, thus preventing you from tabbing to graphical objects such as an input field. In Release 6.11, the invocation option $TABNOPBMENU was added so that it is possible to tab to pixel-based objects. To implement this you need to add the option -$TABNOPB-MENU to the CONFIG.SAS file used at start up.

14

Formats are not always updated from a FRAME

You can create a format from within SCL by using a SUBMIT block with a PROC FORMAT. This is useful in FRAME applications when you wish your application to generate formats interactively. These formats can then be used by your program for displaying data or doing table lookups. This kind of use sometimes requires updating the format which you generate with new data. However, if you try to create a format of the same name to replace your first format, the second format will NOT take effect. Once a format is generated, there is no way to update it from your FRAME application. If you try to, it seems as though it has worked (i.e., no error message); however, when you use the format, you find that it is your original one that is used.

14

Automatic line insert when editing SCL

Ever noticed how in the PROGRAM EDITOR window you can insert a new line simply by pressing the Enter key? I find this much quicker to use than having to use commands such as I (insert) or TS (text split). This behavior is also possible in the SCL source window by issuing the command AUTOSPLIT. You may find that you have to issue this command every time you open the window. I've set a function key to this command to make things easier.

14

Setting the window size of dialog frames

Typically the window size is altered by changing the window size values in the GATTR (general attributes). An easier and quicker way is to use the SETWSZ command.

1. Develop your frame, laying out the widgets as required.

2. Using the mouse, resize the frame to the size you want by clicking and dragging the bottom right corner of the frame.

3. Position the frame where you want it on the screen by using the mouse to click and drag the title bar to the required position.

4. When the frame is the size and is in the position that you require, issue the command SETWSZ. This will set the GATTR windows size values to the values of the currently displayed frame.

14

Ensuring INSERT key is off at start of FRAME entries

It is possible to start an AF application with the INSERT key automatically switched off. There is a display manager command WINSERT ON/OFF. As a DM command, it can be executed by the EXECCMDI SCL function. The easiest way to ensure INSERT is toggled off in an application is to place the following statement in the INIT section of the very first entry of the application.

```
CALL EXECCMDI('WINSERT OFF') ;
```

For more information

See *Microsoft Windows Environment: Changes and Enhancements to the SAS System, Release 6.10*, page 58 and *OS/2 Environment: Changes and Enhancements to the SAS System, Release 6.10*, page 49

Refreshing the Build window

When developing with SAS/AF software, if you have the Build window open and you allocate a new library or change the name of an existing one, then the Build window often does not refresh with the new library information. Entering the command RESET will refresh the window. This command could be assigned to a function key or a toolbar item.

14

Cleaning up in the terminate (Term:) section

Good structured programming practice states that a program should only have one entry point and one exit point. This generated some discussion on the SAS-L newsgroup and some people have different views. Using conditional statements such as _STATUS_='H' immediately halts execution of the current program and exits the program at that point. Normally a program terminates via the terminate section. The purpose of the terminate section is to carry out any housekeeping on exit such as saving data and deleting work data sets and lists. If the _STATUS_='H'; statement is used then the terminate section is by-passed which is undesirable.

When terminating a program, delete any unwanted data sets and lists. This will improve performance. An example of a TERM section that deletes temporary data sets and SCL lists follows:

```
array del{*} $ ('c3', 'c4', 'currdesc', 'currency','external',
'ibnr',
                'local', 'noc3', 'noc4', 'nolimit',
'notfr','notfrc3',
                'np_limit', 'others', 'report', 'repttemp',
'samcotfr',

'sect1','sect2','sect2c3','sect2c4','sect3','teritory',
                'unearned' 'sect1c4');


Term:
*delete temporary datasets;
   do x=1 to dim(del);
     if exist(del{x}) then    do;
        put '        REPT2_12.FRAME Deleting member:' del{x} '
on termination.';
        rc=delete(del{x});
     end;
   end;
*delete temporary SCL lists;
   if listlen(arealid)>=0 then dellist(arealid);
   if listlen(salesplid)>=0 then dellist(salesplid);
return;
```

The deletion of lists is particularly important with OOP as undeleted lists can hog memory. Each time an object is created, used and destroyed, if temporary lists are not deleted, then the usable memory will be eroded away (known as memory leaks). This can severely affect performance.

When writing new classes, or creating subclasses, ensure that temporary lists are deleted in the overriding _TERM_ method. In Release 6.11 there is an automatic clean-up feature. If instance variables have a type of LIST, then they are automatically deleted when the object's _TERM_ method executes.

Making a box look sunken

In SAS/AF frames, you can use GRSEGs (SAS/GRAPH output objects) to alter the appearance of things on the screen. Fill the master region with a GRSEG which you paint with the Graphics Editor. Have gray lines on one side and white on the other, with a gray background. This then gives the appearance of a sunken box.

The steps to do this are:

1. Create a GRSEG (according to the instructions above) in the Graphics Editor, which can be entered by selecting Globals, Present, Create Graphs.

2. Import the GRSEG into a frame as a SAS/GRAPH output object.

Using hotspots on graphs

SAS/GRAPH Output Objects

These objects are powerful and flexible. One of their nice features is that the user can click on parts of a graph and return a value or some information associated with what was clicked on. This enables drill-down to be easily implemented. This is all built into the Graphics object.

You must turn this functionality on by selecting "Turn hotspot mode on" by clicking with the right mouse button on the SAS/GRAPH Output object. A hotspot can either return a value in a variable by using the _GET_VALUE_ method, or it can display data in the DATA INFO window.

NOTE: A Graphics object is different from a SAS/GRAPH object. A Graphics object does not create a GRSEG catalog entry.

SAS/GRAPH output objects are used to display a graph from a SAS/GRAPH catalog entry. The graph may be one created with a PROC or DSGI, or it may have been converted from another format to a GRSEG catalog entry.

Hotspots

These can be invisibly laid over other objects in a frame. When clicked on, they can return information about the object that is clicked on.

What this means

If you have a graph that is too complex to be created by the Graphics object or one that has been created by a PROC or DSGI, then by using a hotspot you can get information about what part of the graph is clicked on and its value.

Example

I overlaid a hotspot on a vertical bar graph which had values along the X-axis. The hotspot only covered the values on the X-axis. So when the user clicked on one of these values, I could use the _GET_VALUE_ method to return which one they clicked on. I then used this value to implement drill-down by displaying a new graph applicable to the value that they selected.

There is a nice method called _GET_INFO_ that can be used in SAS/GRAPH Output Class objects.

14

This method tells you everything an overlaid hotspot could. The method returns a list identifier that contains X,Y coordinates of where the mouse clicked, the text (if any) that was clicked on, and several other useful values.

The relationship between the hotspot and the thing it overlays cannot be guaranteed in some circumstances. If the application is used with a different sized font than your display font, then the sizing of the GRSEG may be different. Your bar may not line up with your hotspot anymore.

For more information

See *SAS/AF Software: FRAME Entry Usage and Reference*, pages 431-432.

Additional SAS documentation

If you want more information about the tips covered in this section, then try reading the relevant SAS documentation.

These manuals include:

- *SAS Screen Control Language: Reference, Version 6, Second Edition*
- *SAS/AF Software: FRAME Application Development Concepts, Version 6, First Edition*
- *Beyond the Obvious with SAS Screen Control Language*
- *Professional SAS User Interfaces*
- *SAS/AF Software: FRAME Class Dictionary, Version 6, First Edition*

14

Chapter 15
SAS/CONNECT® Software

15

Connecting SAS sessions between mainframes

Something that SAS users sometimes misunderstand is that client/server doesn't always mean mainframe to PC. It can mean mainframe to mainframe or almost any platform to any other platform (PC to RS/6000, RS/6000 to HP, HP to MVS, etc.). Where I work, we have SAS/CONNECT available on most of our mainframe systems and on PCs. We run MVS/ESA with a TCP network.

SAS/CONNECT will allow you to make use of 3 types of client/server services. One SAS session becomes the client and another the server.

1. Compute Services are used by using an RSUBMIT function to execute SAS code on the server.

2. Remote Library Services (new in Release 6.08) allow access to remote data libraries, moving data through the network as it is required. The LIBNAME statement would be specified as follows:

LIBNAME *libref* <REMOTE> <*'sas-data-library'*> SERVER=*rsessid* <*engine/host-options*> ;

The server is the remote session ID that you signed on with.

3. Data transfer services move a copy of data from one machine to another; for example, PROC UPLOAD and PROC DOWNLOAD are data transfer procedures.

Example code to establish link between two systems

```
* I have logged onto the mainframe and entered online SAS ;
* Now I tell SAS what protocol I will use to connect ;
* and what system to connect to (you can PING the system to
see if its there) ;
options comamid=tcp
        remote=abc ;
* Now I tell SAS where my SAS/CONNECT logon script is ;
* The logon script tells SAS how to logon to the remote system
;
* filename rlink "ivmktg.xv02341.cntl(tcptso)" ;
* Now I tell SAS to go ahead and log on to the remote system ;
* make sure you are not already logged on to it ;
signon ;
* To cut off the link enter SIGNOFF on the command line.
```

15

Using SAS/CONNECT in batch mode

By default SAS/CONNECT scripts are set up to allow the user to interactively log on to remote systems. However, this can be automated so that the process can occur entirely in batch mode. This allows a SAS batch job to be connected from any mainframe system to any other(s) using SAS/CONNECT. This means that if a system is running out of resources then you can run a program on another system, linking to the one where the data is. (Assuming your network can handle the data traffic)

Here is PROC CONTENTS output that I produced in batch mode, running on one machine and accessing data on another. This example was done from one MVS mainframe running the SAS System to another over a TCP/IP network.

```
                                    CONTENTS PROCEDURE
        ----Directory----
        Libref:                             CHARM
        Engine:                             SASE9
        Physical Name:
        SYS1.PROD.D940715.SASLIB
        Accessed through server:            SY2
        Server's libref:                    SYS00016
        Server's engine:                    V608
        Views interpreted in server's execution: YES
        Unit:                               DISK
        Volume:                             D00107
        Disposition:                        OLD
        Device:                             3380
        Blocksize:                          23040
        Blocks per Track:                   2
        Total Library Blocks:               330
        Total Used Blocks:                  314
        Total Free Blocks:                  16
        Highest Used Block:                 314
        Highest Formatted Block:            314
        Members:                            1


                    #   Name    Memtype   Indexes
                    ---------------------
                    1   CHARM   DATA
```

To get this to work in batch, you need to modify the SAS/CONNECT script, in this case SCRIPT (TCPTSO) which is set up to work in an online environment. Eliminate the script asking for input (INPUT statements) and add the data into the TYPE statements.

15

```
/*————————MVS LOGON————————*/
*   input 'Userid?';
    type 'user0001' LF;
    waitfor 'ENTER ACCOUNT', 30 seconds : nolog;
*    input 'Account?';
    type 'account code 2' LF;
    waitfor 'ENTER CURRENT PASSWORD', 60 seconds : nolog;
*    input nodisplay 'Password?';
    type 'secret1' LF;
```

This is my example JCL. Note the options where the system that you want to connect to is specified. FILENAME points to your script, which must be modified to include your userid, account code and password. Then LIBNAME specifies the system that you are connecting to in SERVER=.

You could link to several mainframes and access the data on each of them in the one program by specifying different SERVER= parameters in various LIBNAME statements.

Screen Shot

```
EDIT — USER0001.XVV1241.CNTL(CONNECT) - 01.75 ————
COLUMNS 001 072
COMMAND ===>                                              SCROLL
===> CSR
****** **************************** TOP OF DATA****************************
000001 //JOBSPM00 JOB 'ACCOUNT001','PM6342306',NOTIFY=&SYSUID,
000002 //          CLASS=U,MSGCLASS=X,MSGLEVEL=(1,1),REGION=2M
000003 //*
000004 //* CONNECT TO SY2
000005 //*
000006 //CONNECT   EXEC SAS
000007 //SYSIN     DD  *
000008 OPTIONS COMAMID=TCP REMOTE=SY2 ;
000009 FILENAME RLINK 'USER000.XVV1241.CNTL(TCPTSO)' ;
000010 SIGNON ;
000011
000012 LIBNAME CHARM SASE9 'SYS1.PROD.D940715.SASLIB'
000013          SERVER=SY2 DISP=SHR ;
000014
000015 PROC CONTENTS DATA=CHARM._ALL_ ;
000016 RUN ;
000017
000018 SIGNOFF ;
****** **************************** BOTTOM OF DATA****************************
```

15

Additional SAS documentation

If you want more information about the tips covered in this section, then try reading the relevant SAS documentation.

These manuals include:

- *SAS/CONNECT Software: Usage and Reference, Version 6, Second Edition*

Chapter 16
MVS Tips

16

16

Some of the tips in this section relate to using the SAS System under the MVS operating system. Other tips in the section apply to MVS in general and apply equally to SAS or any other programs used under MVS.

Questions to always ask yourself

What am I doing to the machine?

Why am I doing it?

Can I do it some better way?

Who can I ask if I am doing things the right way?

Using the ISPF editor from the SAS system

If you prefer the ISPF editor to the SAS program editor, then do the following:

1. Start SAS from within ISPF (for example, TSO SAS).

2. Type HOST on the PROGRAM EDITOR command line.

3. Any text in the PROGRAM EDITOR is transferred to the ISPF editor, and when you END, your edited text is returned to the PROGRAM EDITOR.

The ISPF interface features (including HED) were considered production status from TSLEVEL 425 of Release 6.08.

(Similar functionality exists on other operating systems)

For more information

The current documentation for HOSTEDIT is SAS Technical Report P-266, *Developing ISPF Applications with the SAS System, Release 6.08.*

Listing tape labels from the SAS system

SAS can read tape labels (under MVS) to let you know what files are on your tape or cartridge.

```
PROC TAPELABEL DDNAME= (FILEREF or ddname ...) PAGE;
```

TAPELABEL: Introduction (from SAS Online Help)

One or more standard-labeled tape volumes can be processed by TAPELABEL. Only one volume per job control statement or command is processed; however, multiple job control statements can be used in one job to process more than one tape volume.

The procedure prints information from the tape label, including the data set name, DCB information and data set history.

At some installations if you cannot use LABEL=(,BLP), it may be necessary to specify the data set name of the first file on the tape volume in the job control language that describes the volumes to be processed.

For each file on a tape volume, TAPELABEL prints:

FILE NUMBER	the file sequence number
DSNAME	the data set name
RECFM	the record format
LRECL	the logical record length
BLKSIZE	the block size
BLOCK COUNT	the number of blocks in the file (from trailer label)
EST. FEET	the estimated length of the file in feet
CREATED	the file creation date
EXPIRES	the file expiration date
CREATED BY JOB NAME STEPNAME	the job and step names of the job that created the file
TRTCH	the track recording technique
DEN	the file recording density code
PSWD	the file protection indicator
UHL	the number of user header labels
UTL	the number of user trailer labels

TAPELABEL also prints the sum of the estimated file lengths.

16

Left of Example Output

```
TAPE LIST FOR DD
CONTENTS OF TAPE VOLUME -   810292

                                              BLOCK   EST
  FILE
  NUMBER DSNAME          RECFM  LRECL  BLKSIZE COUNT   FEET

     1    V.CART.VI2.SASLIB  FB    32760   32760  14161   1117.4
                                                          ------
                                                          1117.4
```

Right of Example Output

```
NAME -  TAPE
                                        OWNER -

                        CREATED BY
          CREATED   EXPIRES   JOB NAME STEPNAME  TRTCH  DEN  PSWD  UHL  UTL
18JAN1995 0000099    SAMS5RV2/RECEIVE            P      5    NO    0    0
```

Defining user-defined ISPF commands

Define an application command table to let you make your own commands that can be used anywhere ISPF is used to run programs, commands, panels, etc. To see a list of standard background commands, go into ISPF option 3.9 and enter ISPF as the application ID. This shows the default background commands. You can make your own application commands by making a new table and invoking ISPF with the NEWAPPL(xxx) parm, where xxx is your application ID. Note that you can't modify the default ISP application command table since it is stored in a system table allocated to "everyone".

16

Useful ISPF editing functions

Don't forget these highly useful edit commands: UC and LC for upper- and lowercase (also UCC and LCC); TS and TF for splitting text over two lines or flowing text together (especially useful when assigned to a key as :TS and :TF); the overlay edit command O; the margin commands),)), (, and ((. All these, when used properly, can save an awful lot of editing and typing. For more information, press PF1 when in the edit screen.

16

Check JCL syntax prior to running

Many sites have a standard JCL checker which is invoked by entering !JCK on the command line of the ISPF editor. Checking your JCL saves resources that are otherwise wasted by the system interpreting your JCL, allocating resources, and so on until it abends. This JCL checker picks up many things but not all. For instance, it will not pick up that a JCLLIB statement is needed.

Use QuickRef for online reference

Many sites have an online tool installed called QuickRef. This is invoked by entering QW on the ISPF command line. It provides access to loads of system documentation, including the meaning of system messages. Entering QW *subject*, will search the Quickref database for the subject you want. QW M=*message* will display the meaning of a system message.

Free tapes after use

When using cartridges and tapes, it is usually best to use FREE=CLOSE in your JCL to free the cart/tape when you are finished with it. This makes it available for others to use, for example,

//SAMPLE DD DSN=THIS.IS.A.TAPE,DISP=SHR,FREE=CLOSE

16

Dispense with your LOG data set

Setting the primary pages to 0 in the LOG data set means that it is not created or written to. Therefore, ISPF runs marginally quicker and you no longer see the exit panel.

16

Use best block sizes

All data sets on DASD should have half-track blocking for the most efficient I/O. The maximum for a 3380 is 23476 and 28,300 for a 3390. There are exceptions. For SAS catalogs, a smaller blocksize such as 6144 is advisable in the following cases (see your MVS companion): if your data set or members are smaller than half track, if very few reads or writes are done to the data set, if your job is short on virtual storage (since every DDNAME allocated reserves 5 buffers of block-size, that is, a 23K block-size will use 115K of virtual storage). On a 3090 each IO costs about 3,000 instructions. 1 CPU second is about 3,000 I/Os. To save 1 CPU second, reduce the I/Os by 3,000. Blocksize on tapes should be as large as possible - ie. 32,756. For SMS, specifying BLKSIZE=0 uses system determined block-size. This gives the optimum block size for your data set, providing you specify DSORG and RECFM.

16

Obtaining a big region size

Asking for a REGION=0M will give the maximum region size available on the machine you are on. It is best to ask for the minimum storage that your job requires (see SASLOG) which will avoid potential problems with excessive paging. Running a job once with a large region size to find out how much memory is required and then running with the right size specified is recommended.

Remember that this has little or no effect on SAS unless the MEMSIZE SAS system option is also used.

16

Use VIO for small temporary files

Use VIO for small temporary files (UNIT=VIO). This ensures data sets created and re-read in a job stay in pageable memory and do no physical I/O, apart from paging. Don't put a file bigger than 10 megabyte in VIO or excessive paging will occur. Don't use VIO for sort work areas. If you have SMS, it should automatically switch all small temporary files to VIO.

16

Invoke user CLISTs with the % prefix

Use % in front of any CLIST command. This makes the CLIST quicker by removing the search for the CLIST through your STEPLIBs, Linkpack and LINKLIST, and by directing the search straight to the SYSPROC DD statement. Libraries located under the SYSPROC DD are where user commands are usually located.

16

Examine EXCP counts

Examine the EXCPs done to various files/DDnames. This information can be gained by installing a job exit, examining SMF records (in MICS or MXG database), looking in the JESLOG, etc. Once you know the data sets with a lot of activity, you can look at blocking, buffering, or keeping the data in storage to help reduce activity. For a small data set with many I/Os, use UNIT=VIO rather than UNIT=SYSDA. This can substantially reduce the elapsed time of your job. Read small lookup tables into storage and read them there rather than looking them up in a file every time. Using a format for lookup makes use of this technique.

Remember that you can also specify OPTIONS FULLSTIMER in SAS, which will provide extra statistics on the resources used by each DATA or PROC step.

16

Use the appropriate batch job classes

Use the correct job class for the job. Particularly try to make use of the overnight job class, which is cheaper and removes load on the system during the day.

16

Use batch rather than online TSO

Use batch mode rather than online mode for long commands, for example, LISTCATs. Batch is more efficient, and your terminal is not tied up for a long time waiting for a response.

16

Browse rather than edit

Use BROWSE rather than EDIT. This is especially true for large data sets. EDIT copies the whole data set into main storage in your address space; BROWSE copies only the first block into your address space.

Chaining ISPF commands

If you know your next sequence of commands, enter them all at once by either using 1.2.3.4 to go to option 4 in option 3 in option 2 in option 1, or by chaining your commands with semicolons. In some systems, such as Infoman, you should use commas to chain commands.

You can also assign commands to function keys. In this way a number of commands can be invoked at the press of a key.

Copying files

Use IEBGENER to copy sequential files not IDCAMS REPRO (which is very inefficient). If you have ICEGENER or SSGENER use that instead since it is more efficient that IEB-GENER.

16

Pre-processing ISPF panels

Pre-process your panel libraries by using the ISPPREP command (entered on the command line when coding a panel) to speed them up. This is especially useful for long and complicated panels. If you do this, realize that the source code is not kept.

Library concatenations

Avoid having lots of ISPxLIBs allocated when you logon. For example, every time a panel is requested, each library is searched in turn for that panel. The more libraries there are to search, the slower the response time, especially when the panel you want is in the last library. Reducing the number of libraries allocated will reduce the response time at logon time also. Putting the busiest libraries first in the concatenation will help. However, the most active libraries are usually the system libraries, which means it is difficult to have your own versions of system panels or CLISTs.

Keep JCL and source separate

Keep JCL and source in separate PDS members. If they are together in the same member, JES has to process the data three times, rather than just once if the program or data is read in directly from a PDS or data set. The data is processed once at read time, once at converter/interpreter time, and once when the data is actually required.

Log off when you're finished

Log off when you are finished so that you free up the storage that your userid was using. If you are using NETMASTER, use the NETMASTER of the system (or site) where you are going to do most of your work. This cuts down on network traffic.

16

Do not keep pressing Enter

Don't keep pressing Enter to see if your job has finished. Give it a chance to run. Every time you press Enter, you cause some action at the host which adds to system load. Another example: if you want to insert 20 lines then use I20 rather than inserting one line and pressing Enter to get 19 new ones.

16

Additional SAS documentation

If you want more information about the tips covered in this section, then try reading the relevant SAS documentation.

These manuals include:

- *Getting Started with the SAS System in the MVS Environment, Version 6, First Edition*
- *SAS Companion for the MVS Environment, Version 6, Second Edition*
- *Tuning SAS Applications in the MVS Environment*

Index

A

ampersand (&), format modifier
64

arrays
bounds 60–61
defining 59
initial values 61
multi-dimensional 60
number of elements 60
passing by reference 212–213
referencing 59
temporary 61

asterisk (*)
as wildcard 5
in CATLIST function 206
in pattern matching 48

AUTOEXEC.BAT, logging 27

AUTOSCROLL setting 15

AUTOSPLIT command 236

AWS (SAS Application Workspace
window)
sizing 8
turning off menu bar 8

B

batch jobs, determining currently
executing 102

batch vs. TSO 272

block sizes, optimal 266

BROWSE vs. EDIT command
273

Build window, refreshing 239

BXOR function 9–10

BY groups
formatting reports with 169
page eject after 121
PROC steps vs. DATA steps
83–85

BY statement
merge results 86–87
vs. CLASS statement 156–158

BY variables, in titles 121

C

CALCULATED keyword 195

CALL EXECUTE statement 49–50

CALL LABEL function 76–77

CANCEL command, detecting
207–208

CANCEL option 78

case, changing in ISPF editor
261

case consistency in SCL constant
names 218

case sensitivity, DATA step 65

catalog members, determining
space used 133

catalogs, selection list of 206

CATLIST function 206

CLASS statement vs. BY
statement 156–158

client/server services 249

CLISTs, invoking 269

CLM option 159–160

COALESCE function 194

colon (:)
as a wildcard 4
format modifier 64
in pattern matching 48

commands
AUTOSPLIT 236
BROWSE vs. EDIT 273
CANCEL, detecting 207–208
DELLIST 215
END, detecting 207–208
ISPPREP 276
REMOTE 219
RESET 239
SETWSZ 237
SYSITEMS 57–58

commands, ISPF
chaining 274
list of 261
user-defined 260

comment delimiters (//* *//)
in macro comments 108–109

Call your local SAS office to order these books
from **Books by Users** Press

support.sas.com/pubs

SAS® Functions by Example
by **Ron Cody** . . . . Order No. A59343

SAS® Macro Programming Made Easy
by **Michele M. Burlew** . . . . Order No. A56516

SAS® Programming by Example
by **Ron Cody**
and **Ray Pass** . . . . Order No. A55126

SAS® Programming for Researchers and
Social Scientists, Second Edition
by **Paul E. Spector** . . . . Order No. A58784

SAS® Survival Analysis Techniques for Medical
Research, Second Edition
by **Alan B. Cantor** . . . . Order No. A58416

SAS® System for Elementary Statistical Analysis,
Second Edition
by **Sandra D. Schlotzhauer**
and **Ramon C. Littell** . . . . Order No. A55172

SAS® System for Mixed Models
by **Ramon C. Littell, George A. Milliken, Walter W.
Stroup,** and **Russell D. Wolfinger** . . Order No. A55235

SAS® System for Regression, Second Edition
by **Rudolf J. Freund**
and **Ramon C. Littell** . . . . Order No. A56141

SAS® System for Statistical Graphics, First Edition
by **Michael Friendly** . . . . Order No. A56143

The SAS® Workbook and Solutions Set
(books in this set also sold separately)
by **Ron Cody** . . . . Order No. A55594

Selecting Statistical Techniques for Social Science
Data: A Guide for SAS® Users
by **Frank M. Andrews, Laura Klem, Patrick M. O'Malley,
Willard L. Rodgers, Kathleen B. Welch,**
and **Terrence N. Davidson** . . . . Order No. A55854

Statistical Quality Control Using the SAS® System
by **Dennis W. King** . . . . Order No. A55232

A Step-by-Step Approach to Using the SAS® System
for Factor Analysis and Structural Equation Modeling
by **Larry Hatcher** . . . . Order No. A55129

A Step-by-Step Approach to Using the SAS® System
for Univariate and Multivariate Statistics
by **Larry Hatcher**
and **Edward Stepanski** . . . . Order No. A55072

Step-by-Step Basic Statistics Using SAS®: Student
Guide and Exercises
(books in this set also sold separately)
by **Larry Hatcher** . . . . Order No. A57541

Survival Analysis Using the SAS® System:
A Practical Guide
by **Paul D. Allison** . . . . Order No. A55233

Tuning SAS® Applications in the OS/390 and z/OS
Environments, Second Edition
by **Michael A. Raithel** . . . . Order No. A58172

Univariate and Multivariate General Linear Models:
Theory and Applications Using SAS® Software
by **Neil H. Timm**
and **Tammy A. Mieczkowski** . . . . Order No. A55809

Using SAS® in Financial Research
by **Ekkehart Boehmer, John Paul Broussard,**
and **Juha-Pekka Kallunki** . . . . Order No. A57601

Using the SAS® Windowing Environment:
A Quick Tutorial
by **Larry Hatcher** . . . . Order No. A57201

Visualizing Categorical Data
by **Michael Friendly** . . . . Order No. A56571

Web Development with SAS® by Example
by **Frederick Pratter** . . . . Order No. A58694

Your Guide to Survey Research Using the
SAS® System
by **Archer Gravely** . . . . Order No. A55688

support.sas.com/pubs

JMP® Books

JMP® Start Statistics, Third Edition
by **John Sall, Ann Lehman,**
and **Lee Creighton** . . . . Order No. A58166

Regression Using JMP®
by **Rudolf J. Freund, Ramon C. Littell,**
and **Lee Creighton** . . . . Order No. A58789